KARL BARTH'S
DOCTRINE OF ELECTION

KARL BARTH'S DOCTRINE OF ELECTION

WILLIAM JOHN HAUSMANN
Drew University

PHILOSOPHICAL LIBRARY
New York

15 East 40th Street, New York, New York 10016

Library of Congress Catalog Card No. 74-81812
Manufactured in the United States of America

TABLE OF CONTENTS

KARL BARTH'S
DOCTRINE OF ELECTION

INTRODUCTION

I. Definition of the Problem of the Thesis—area of investigation.

1. *The Christological Content of Karl Barth's Doctrine of Election.*

The theology of Karl Barth claims to be strict Christological thinking. In other words, every doctrine in Barth's theological system has its point of departure in the Person and Work of Jesus Christ. In fact, as Hartwell points out, the christological concentration of the "Church Dogmatics," and indeed of Barth's theology as a whole, is "unparalleled in the history of Christian thought." [1] Barth's doctrine of election is not only christologically oriented but offers a specific Christology which radically departs from the various traditional Christologies in the history of Christian doctrine.

Karl Barth's doctrine of Election stands or falls with this Christology, that is, with the place and function of Jesus Christ in God's decree of Election. There are, according to Barth, three aspects to the function of Jesus Christ in the decree of Election:

a. Jesus Christ is Himself the Electing God.
b. Jesus Christ is the Elect Man.
c. Jesus Christ is the only Man rejected or damned by God.

This is the substance of Barth's doctrine of Election. These three statements are identity statements corresponding to Barth's concept of "Double Predestination." This means that Jesus Christ who is the Electing God and the Elect Man and therefore who is the only Man rejected by

God has elected Himself to damnation and man to salvation. This further means that Jesus Christ is not merely the mirror of Election, the Mediator or Executor but is Himself the very Decree of Election. Thus Barth has significantly departed from Calvinism and Reformed Orthodoxy in this doctrine.

In this thesis we will have to investigate Barth's concept of the place or function of Jesus Christ in God's decree of Election. This is the christological problem of Barth's doctrine of Election.

2. *The relationship of the rejection of Jesus Christ to the rejection of individual men.*

In this thesis we are mainly concerned with Barth's view that since Jesus Christ is both the subject and object of God's decree of Election, He is therefore the only Man rejected by God. We are mainly interested in the question of the relationship of the rejection and damnation of Jesus Christ to the rejection and damnation of individual men. According to Barth we must have a christological understanding of the rejection or damnation, of the ultimate destiny, of the individual man. Barth makes a distinction between what it means for Jesus Christ to be rejected and what it means for individual men to be rejected by God.

There are three sections to this thesis. First, we will investigate Barth's points of departure from the main traditional positions of the Church as reflected by Athanasius, Augustine, Thomas Aquinas, Luther, Calvin, Reformed and Lutheran theology on the question of Election and Reprobation. Secondly, we will investigate Barth's own solutions to the problem of Election and Reprobation. Thirdly, we will present a critical analysis of Barth's own theological methodology and the christological content of his view that Jesus Christ is the only man rejected by God.

II. The Problem of a Correct Doctrine of the Election of Grace.

1. *Barth's Identification of Election and Grace.*

Barth's doctrine of Election is actually his understanding of the Gospel, that is, his understanding or interpretation of God's eternal plan for salvation for mankind. In

Barth's doctrine of Election we are confronted with his understanding of the true meaning of Grace, and of all the ways and works of God. Thus the doctrine of Election is not simply for Barth one doctrine in a series of doctrines in Barth's theology in general or in his "Church Dogmatics" in particular. Barth identifies Election with Grace, with the Gospel, with the content of the message of salvation as he emphatically declares in his "Church Dogmatics":

> The doctrine of election is the sum of the Gospel because of all words that can be said or heard it is the best: that God elects man, that God is for man too the One who loves in freedom. It is grounded in the knowledge of Jesus Christ because He is both the electing God and elected man in One. It is part of the doctrine of God because originally God's election of man is a predestination not merely of man but of Himself. Its function is to bear basic testimony to eternal, free and unchanging grace as the beginning of all the ways and works of God.[2]

In this formal definition of Barth there is no conflict or tension between Election and Grace. This is in sharp contrast to the view of Garrigou-Lagrange who points out two difficulties in the "Problem of Predestination" as he refers to it:

a. The first difficulty is how to reconcile Predestination with God's will to save all mankind.[3]

This has been a continuing problem in the history of Christian thought. In the formal definition of Election given by Barth we do not find any such problem or any attempt to reconcile Predestination with God's will to save mankind. For Barth the two, Predestination or Election and God's Will, are one or identical.

b. The second difficulty relates to the problem of the eternal destiny of individuals, the elect and the non-elect. Why has God predestined this individual to be among the elect or saved and another individual to be among the non-elect or lost or eternally damned? Why has God chosen Peter to be saved rather than Judas, and not vice versa?[4]

Again, in his formal definition of Election Barth does

not speak of two groups of individuals, of the elect and the non-elect, but rather of God's election of men. Thus Barth's doctrine of the Election of Grace affects his understanding of the nature of God and the destiny of men. This is further reflected in defining God more precisely by speaking of Jesus Christ as the electing God. Barth defines Election, Grace, God and Salvation christologically. In dealing with the problem of the individual Barth defines the individual christologically, both his election and rejection. For Barth the object of election is not two groups of individuals but God and man as christologically defined. In Jesus Christ God and man are elected or are the objects of election. This is Barth's unique understanding of the doctrine of the Election of Grace which affects the whole body of Christian doctrine.

2. *Christological Form or Christological Content?*

Does Barth's doctrine of Election have true christological content? Or does it merely have christological form? Is there a sound exegetical basis for Barth's christological understanding of Election and Reprobation? Can Barth harmonize the function of Jesus Christ as the only Man rejected by God with the New Testament presentation of Jesus Christ as the Judge of all men at the end of history or at the final Judgment? Is there a logical inconsistency in Barth's doctrine of Election when he refuses to identify his position with that of Universalism and speaks of the possibility of rejection and damnation? The thesis of Barth that Jesus Christ is the only Man rejected by God is a richly varied and complex conception. Barth does not intend this statement that Jesus Christ is the only man rejected by God to be understood as another principle or abstract statement.

Barth's methodology and christological thinking offer a number of possibilities or solutions to the question of the damnation of individual men. Barth challenges us to rethink the whole question of the meaning of damnation or rejection in the Doctrine of Election in the light of Jesus Christ as the electing God, the elect Man and the only Man rejected by God.

In this thesis I propose to investigate Barth's thesis that Jesus Christ is the only Man rejected by God to see whether or not Barth's approach and proposed solutions throw further light on the meaning of rejection and damnation, whether Barth has an advantage over the various traditions in the history of Christian thought on this question and whether his christological approach gives a better foundation to the whole question of the rejection and damnation of individual men.

Chapter I

THE PROBLEM OF THE PLACE OF THE DOCTRINE OF ELECTION IN SYSTEMATIC THEOLOGY

The Place of Election in Other Theological Systems in the History of Christian Thought

1. *Election in relation to Providence and Creation.*

Where the doctrine of Election stands in relation to the other doctrines in a theological system reveals the significance that this doctrine has. Barth's theology which is christologically oriented, and whose Christology is an election Christology and whose doctrine of Election reveals the identity of Election with Grace, and which identifies Grace with the will of God and the will of God with the Gospel, determines the place of the doctrine of Election in his theological system of thought.

Barth gives us a systematic review of the place of Election in past theological systems of thought and then on the basis of his christological orientation he departs from these previous arrangements of the place of Election in systematic theology and charts a new course.

In his theological system Calvin joined Predestination to the doctrine of Creation and the doctrine of Providence.[5] In the system of Thomas Aquinas as contained in the *Summa Theologica* the doctrine of election is joined to the doctrine of divine providence.[6] In Zwingli's *Fidei ratio* (1530) the doctrine of Election forms the crown and completion of the doctrine of Providence.[7] In the Orthodoxy of Reformed Theology in the seventeenth century the doctrine of Predestination followed closely upon the doctrine of God, preceding the doctrine of Creation.[8] Barth does not follow the Reformed Tradition because it was rather the tenet of the decrees of God in general which took precedence over that of Election.[9] This view of Reformed Theology was closely related to the view of Thomas Aquinas which understood Election as connected with Providence.[10]

2. *Election in relation to Christology and Creation.*

Barth points out that one theological system speaks first of Creation and Providence and then only, in greater or lesser proximity, of the Election as over against the Reformed scheme. Barth takes note of a small but interesting group in which the Christology followed directly upon the doctrine of God, being succeeded by Creation and then Predestination.

This system is found among the older Lutherans such as J. Gerhard *Loci theol;* 1610f. who brings out the direct consequence God-Christ-Providence-Predestination. In the case of L. Hutterus *Comp. Loc. theol.* (1610) we find that between the doctrines of Creation and Predestination he has intersected those of sin, the Law, the Gospel and Justification.

Barth's objection is that those who advocated this arrangement allowed Christology to displace the doctrine of Election, instead of filling it out and giving it form. The advocates co-ordinated Election with that of Creation and Providence and even subordinated Election to them.[11]

3. *Election in relation to Reconciliation.*

Here there are a number of possibilities and arrangements. There is the view that the Election of Grace is quite clearly detached from the doctrine of God and treated after the doctrine of Creation and even after that of Sin. The result is that the doctrine of Election is detached equally from the doctrine of Providence, and instead brought into direct connection with the doctrine of Reconciliation.[12]

Three other arrangements in different ways seek to present Predestination as the principle and key to the whole of Reconciliation, or Soteriology, related to the Church as the place where Atonement between God and man is actualized. Predestination follows immediately after Christology. This was the method chosen by Calvin in the first draft of his Catechism (1537), and later by Peter Martyr in his *Loci Communes* (1576).[13]

A second possibility is that the doctrine of Election is related to sin and has precedence over Christology as well as Soteriology. This arrangement we find in Calvin *Conf. Gallicana* (1559), John Knox *Conf. Scotica (*1560*)*, *Conf. Belgica (*1561*)*, H. Bullinger's *Conf. Helv. post.* (1562), and the *Summa Theologicae* of J. Coccejus (1662). The third possibility is that the doctrine of Election in some degree is the consummation of that of Reconciliation. This we find in Calvin's *Institutio* (1539-1554) and in A. Calov's *Systema loc. theol.*

Barth's criticism is that these arrangements make the doctrine of Election supplementary and secondary to the doctrine of Reconciliation.[14]

4. *Election in relation to the Church.*

Barth does not mention Francis Pieper, a past theologian of the Lutheran Church-Missouri Synod (of which the writer of this Thesis is presently a member) who presents another possibility or arrangement but one with which Barth would not agree. Pieper took the position that the doctrine of Election came after the doctrine of the Church because Scripture addresses those who by faith have become members of the Christian Church as the elect (Eph. 1:3ff; 2 Thess. 2:13-14, etc.). He further preferred this position for the reason that Scripture assigns to the doctrine of Election not a principal, but an auxiliary role. It served to corroborate the doctrine of Salvation by Grace alone.[15]

To this view of Pieper, Barth would object that the Electing God comes before the elect people. There is no such thing as an assurance of faith apart from the electing God.[16]

Barth's New Arrangement of the Place of the Doctrine of Election in His Theological System As Contained in the *Church Dogmatics*

1. *Election and God.*

Barth does not follow the above arrangements in the history of Christian thought with respect to the doctrine of Election, nor does he, like Pieper, regard the doctrine of Election as serving in an auxiliary role. Instead he has connected the doctrine of Election with the doctrine of God and has given it a precedence over all the other individual tenets of the Christian faith relating to the work of God.

No previous dogmatician has adopted such a course. Barth deals with Election before Creation, before the work of Reconciliation, before eternal Redemption.[17]

The reason why Barth cannot separate Election from the doctrine of God as do the other arrangements is because God is the Electing God, the Subject of Election. To connect Election with the doctrine of creation or providence would be to begin with an unknown God, a God in general, the absolute World-Ruler, with an abstract god. Election, according to Barth, is not one of the many functions of world-government. God is not a first cause. Such a God is an abstract god. Barth will have nothing to do with such a concept of God.[18]

In place of the abstract God Barth speaks of the concrete God. He says that we must know first who this ruler is and what He wills and does in that rule. We must know who God is before we can speak of His ways and works in Creation and Providence. And this concrete aspect of His rule results from a consideration of the concept of Election. We know who and what God is in the doctrine of Election.[19]

Therefore our knowledge of God, of His nature and works, depends upon our knowing God as the electing God. Barth goes so far as to say that there can be no subsequent knowledge of God, whether from His revelation or from His work as disclosed in that revelation, which is not as such knowledge of this Election. There can be no Christian truth which does not from the very first contain within itself as its basis the fact that from and to all eternity God is the electing God.[20]

2. *Election and Jesus Christ.*

It is not enough merely to know that God is the electing God. Barth maintains that if we would know who God is, and what is the meaning and purpose of His election, and in what respect He is the electing God, then we must look away from all others, and excluding all side-glances or secondary thoughts, we must look only upon and to the name of Jesus Christ, and the existence and history of the people of God enclosed within Him.[21]

There is christological content in the concept of God as the electing God in Barth's doctrine of Election. It is Christology, election Christology, that determines the relation of the doctrine of Election to the other doctrines in Barth's system of theological thought. In this respect the other theological systems erred according to Barth because Jesus Christ was not considered first and thus ended up with an abstract deity instead of a concrete christological concept of God.

3. *Election and Man.*

Barth warns against a view of man that leaves man equally as abstract as the abstract God. In theology whether man be regarded as a creature, as a sinner or as a Christian he is never outside the sphere of the divine decision. Man is not outside the sphere of the Election of Grace.[22]

According to Barth, then, the other arrangements of the place of the doctrine of Election in Theology distort the doctrine of God, Christ, Man and salvation. Barth intends to correct the situation by means of the christological orientation of the doctrine of Election which makes of this doctrine a principal tenet of the Christian faith.

Chapter II

BARTH'S REJECTION OF THE VARIOUS VIEWS, PRINCIPLES AND SYSTEMS IN THE VARIOUS TRADITIONS OF THE CHURCH REGARDING THE DOCTRINE OF ELECTION

The Christological Errors of Previous Theologians

1. *Barth's christological break with the previous traditional systems of the doctrine of Election.*

The history of doctrine shows that there have been a number of conflicting theological views regarding the meaning of the doctrine of Election. Loraine Boettner points out that this doctrine of Predestination has perhaps raised a greater storm of opposition, and has doubtless been more misrepresented and caricatured than any other doctrine in the Scriptures.[23] Boettner states that there are really only three systems which claim to set forth a way of salvation through Christ:

> a. *Universalism*: This system holds that Christ died for all men and that eventually all shall be saved, either in this life or through a future probation.[24] Barth's system seems to contain a kind of universalism and yet as we shall see later Barth is not a universalist in the usual sense of the term. We could better describe his position as *Christological Universalism.*
>
> b. *Arminianism:* This system holds that Christ died equally and indiscriminately for every individual of mankind, for those who perish no less than for those who are saved; that Election is not an eternal and unconditional act of God; man may receive or reject the Grace of God and successfully resist the regenerating power of the Holy Spirit. It is

possible for man to throw away his salvation and perish eternally.[25] This system is further away from Barth because here there is no conception of God as the electing God and man as elect. It makes a man's salvation dependent upon his will rather than upon God's.

c. *Calvinism:* This system holds that as a result of the fall into sin all men in themselves are guilty, corrupted, hopelessly lost, that from this fallen mass God sovereignly elects some to salvation through Christ, while passing by others, that Christ is sent to redeem His people by a purely substitutionary atonement; that the Holy Spirit efficaciously applies this redemption to the elect, and that all of the elect are infallibly brought to salvation.[26] Barth must reject this view because it denies that Grace is the beginning of all the ways and works of God and posits a dual will in God. He rejects these various systems of salvation through Christ because they are not truly christological, they are only christological in form but not in content.

Barth views the history of the doctrine of Election in terms of the relationship between Predestination and Christology. He asks the question whether there was continuity between these two doctrines in the work or writings of the older theologians and whether they expounded Predestination in the light of Christology and whether they understood Jesus Christ to be the substance of Predestination.[27]

It is Barth's conviction that the older exponents of the doctrine of Election did not see any such continuity of Christology and Predestination in this way. They separated God from Christ in the sense that the work of God in Jesus Christ was one thing and the eternal presupposing of that work was another. They did not acknowledge God and Jesus Christ to be identical. By distorting the doctrine of God they distorted both Christology and Predestination. They viewed man as an object of Predestination only in terms of man in general, or as the race as a whole, as the sum total of individuals. It was not man as the one who is identical with Jesus Christ.[28]

Barth's break with the views, traditions, systems and

theologies of the past is a "christological break" as he himself states it:

> We must not dream of any other God or any other man. We must not seek to know about God or man except as we look on Jesus Christ.[29]

2. *Barth's christological critique of Athanasius and Augustine in their view of Election.*

a. *Barth's points of christological agreement with Athanasius and Augustine.*

In Athanasius Barth finds a theologian representing one of the earliest phases of Church tradition who more nearly expresses his own position on Election. Barth finds that the system of Athanasius contained the three elements of the Electing God, the Elect Man and the Divine Decree of Salvation. Athanasius viewed the being of the eternal Word or Son as such and the reality of the elected man Jesus together with the Election of those who believe in Him. The Election of the man Jesus and our Election have their foundation in the eternity of the Word or Son, an eternity which differs not at all from that of the Father. Athanasius further ascribed to the eternal Word or Son of God a determination towards the elected man Jesus and towards the Election of believers in Him as they are enclosed in Him.

Barth further discovers that Athanasius had not only a conception of the pure being of the Triune God on the one hand, and a conception of the concrete temporal history of salvation willed and fulfilled by God on the other, but over and above that he had also a conception of the concrete decree of salvation made in the bosom of the triune Godhead, and a conception of the Johannine Logos which was identical with Jesus and which was in the beginning with God. Barth believes that Athanasius had a truly Christian conception of the divine decree. For Athanasius this decree, or Predestination, or Election, was in fact, the decision reached at the beginning of all things, at the beginning of the relationship between God and the reality which is distinct from Him. The Subject of this decision is the Triune God—the Son of God no less than the Father and the Holy Spirit, and the specific object of it is the Son of God in His determination as the Son of Man, the God-Man, Jesus

Christ, who is as such the eternal basis of the whole divine Election.[30]

Barth's reference to Athanasius' system of thought on the doctrine of Election makes us doubt the accuracy of Emil Brunner's statement or historical judgment that prior to Augustine there was no doctrine of Predestination.[31] In presenting Athanasius' views on Election Barth discovers a christological approach to the doctrine of Election similar to his own approach and understanding of the doctrine of Election. At this point we can say that there is one outstanding theologian in the history of doctrine who lends support to Barth's christological approach to the doctrine of Election.

As Barth has a christological approach to the concept of Grace so Augustine also regards Jesus Christ as the Most Illustrious Instance of Predestination and we see the meaning of Grace in the Election of Jesus Christ as Augustine himself writes:

> Moreover, the most illustrious Light of predestination and grace is the Savior Himself—the Mediator Himself between God and men, the man Christ Jesus. And, pray, by what preceding merits of its own, whether of works or of faith, did the human nature which is in Him procure for itself that it should be this? Let this have an answer, I beg. That man, whence did He deserve this—to be assumed by the Word coeternal with the Father into unity or person, and be the only-begotten Son of God? Was it because any kind of goodness in Him preceded? What did He do before? What did He believe? What did He ask, that He should attain to this unspeakable excellence? Was it not by the act and the assumption of the Word that that man, from the time He began to be, began to be the only Son of God? [32]

b. *Barth's christological point of departure from Athanasius and Augustine.*

Even though both Athanasius and Augustine speak of the Son of God as the Electing God and Jesus as the Elect Man, they appear to make a sharp distinction between eternity and time, between the Son of God before the Incarnation and the Son of God in the incarnate state or mode of existence. According to them the Eternal Word takes precedent over the Man Jesus or over His humanity. Barth on the other hand speaks of the Divine-human Reality as existing in some sense before the Incarnation. Barth speaks of Election as an act in eternity. The Electing God and the Elect Man are one in eternity. An essential aspect of Barth's doctrine of Election is the pre-existence of the God-Man Jesus Christ and not merely the pre-existence of the Son of God as the Eternal Word.

In the matter of the divine decree of Salvation Barth speaks of Jesus Christ as the only man rejected by God. Barth believes that in the matter of the divine decree Augustine has moved away from the Biblical testimony because Augustine wanted to know why some believe and are saved, and others do not believe and are damned. Augustine found the answer for his view in his interpretation of certain texts in Romans 9, in the fact of a double divine decision from all eternity, i.e., a decision with two parallel sides. Barth rejects Augustine's view of the divine decree because he believes that Augustine has no Biblical or inherent authority for relating God's dealing in this way, as though we had to look at God's Work here and His work there and to understand them as a unity in order to find the premise for this inter-relationship. Barth firmly believes that there is no such double divine decree in Holy Scripture.[33]

Barth's judgment on Augustine is not a severe one because he believes that Augustine checked himself on this matter. On the whole, Augustine avoided reducing God's twofold dealings to one common denominator, even in concept. By *praedestinatio* Augustine almost always understood *praedestinatio ad gratiam* (a definition taken over by Peter Lombard). And therefore *praedestinatio ad vitam.* Predestination consists positively in Election and does not include *reprobatio* according to Barth.[34]

There has been some question as to whether Augustine created a new system or simply taught what the Church of his day taught. Faber maintains that there was a System of Election received and taught by the earliest Church of the two first centuries.[35] Whereas Brunner denied a doctrine of Election before Augustine, Faber maintains that there was one. Faber also maintains that the Catholic Church did not hold Augustine's peculiar views of Election and Reprobation.[36] According to Faber Augustine discovered a system on his own which was entirely different from that of the Church.[37]

H. Richard Niebuhr's judgment agrees with Faber that in Augustine's predestinarian form of the doctrine of Election, Augustine changed his fundamental insight that God chooses men to love him before men love God, into the proposition that God chooses some men and rejects others. So the glorious vision of the City of God turns into a vision of two cities, composed of different individuals, forever separate.[38]

Barth rejects dualism in respect to a God whose decree is a double one and in respect to man whose fate or eternal destiny is a double one: salvation or damnation. Therefore he rejects Augustine's theological and anthropological Dualism.

3. *Barth's christological critique of Aquinas' view of the Election of Jesus Christ.*

a. *Aquinas' view of the Election of the man Jesus.*

In his investigation of the system of Aquinas Barth discovers that he does not speak of Jesus Christ as the Electing God in his doctrine of Election as do Athanasius and Augustine. Aquinas restricted the Election of Jesus Christ to a passive relationship, and thus to His human nature.[39]

Thomas put the emphasis on Jesus Christ as the Elect man. In this way Thomas, according to Barth, had overlooked the relation between the eternal Godhead of Christ which needs no election and His elected humanity. The being of Christ is in the beginning with God, the act of the good-pleasure of God by which the fulness of the Godhead is allowed to dwell in Him, the covenant which God made with Himself and which is for that reason eternal, the oath which God swore by Himself in the interests of man.[40]

Here Barth presents his unique understanding of the relation between the Electing God and the Elect Man in eternity prior to the incarnation. Thomas separated the Elect Man from the Electing God. To speak as does Thomas is to have knowledge only of the Election of the man Jesus as such, and not of the Election and personal electing of the Son of God which precedes this Election. And once again there is danger, Barth warns, of making the Election of Grace a divine mystery detached from the person of Jesus Christ.[41]

Barth points out that not only Thomas Aquinas but also many others after him spoke of the Election of Jesus Christ only in this second and passive sense, and with reference only to the man Jesus.[42]

Thomas' view then was a deterioration of the Athanasian-Augustinian view of the relationship between eternity and time, God and man, Christ's Deity and humanity in the act of Election.

b. *Barth's christological critique of Aquinas' view of the relation of Jesus Christ to God's Decree.*

Barth identifies Jesus Christ with God's Decree of Salvation and teaches that the Election of Jesus Christ is our Election. Thomas also taught that the Election of Jesus Christ is, in fact, the revelation of our Election. In His Election we can and should recognize our own Election.[43]

However, Thomas does not identify Jesus Christ with God's Decree. Thomas says: "praedestinatio nostra ex simplici voluntate Dei dependet." This means that he rests like Calvin upon the *decretum absolutum,* an absolute decree of God instead of the concrete decree. Barth says that Thomas can even hazard the outrageous statement: "Si Christus non fuisset incarnandus, Deus praeordinasset homines salvari per aliam causam." Against this view that God might have ordained men to salvation by some other cause even if Christ had not become incarnate, Barth maintains that only if Jesus Christ is the true and incontestable basis of our Election can He be the basis of our knowledge of the Election and only then can we have any assurance of our own Election.[44]

c. *Barth's christological critique of Aquinas' view of the relation between Election and Reprobation.*

Thomas does not speak of Election and Reprobation as some kind of parallel activity of God or as having the same cause as Augustine found in the will of God. Thomas regarded Reprobation as in fact a separate genus, quite apart from and standing to some extent only in the shadow of *praedestinatio.*[45]

According to Thomas Predestination is a kind of type of the ordering of some persons towards eternal salvation existing in the divine mind.[46] Thus, God from all eternity prepared by Predestination and conceived the idea of the order of some towards salvation.[47] In asking the question whether God reprobates any man, Aquinas answers that God does reprobate some. Through the Providence of God some men are ordained to eternal life and likewise it is part of that Providence to permit some men to fall away from that end, this is called Reprobation.[48] But this is not Double Predestination. Thomas does not teach an Election to salvation and an Election to damnation. Reprobation includes the will to permit a person to fall into sin, and to impose the punishment of damnation on account of that sin.[49] The cause of Reprobation according to Thomas lies in a man's sin, in his free choice to reject Grace. Thomas subordinates Reprobation to Election:

> Reprobation differs in its causality from predestination. This latter is the cause both of what is expected in the future life by the predestined—namely, glory—and of what is received in this life—namely, grace. Reprobation, however, is not the cause of abandonment by God. It is the cause, however, of what is assigned in the future—namely, eternal punishment. But guilt proceeds from the free choice of the person who is reprobated and deserted by grace.[50]

Farrelly observes that Thomas makes a distinction between God's antecedent and consequent will. Antecedent to his consideration of all the particular circumstances, God wills that all men be saved; but consequent upon such consideration, he wills to reprobate some men. In other words, he does not choose them for eternal life.[51]

Barth, however, teaches that Grace is the beginning of all the ways and works of God and is identified with the Election of Jesus Christ and that God's Yes to man is also His last word. According to Thomas God's No to man, while not a part of God's original will and not a part of God's decree in eternity, is allowed in God's providential ordering of things to limit God's Yes, God's Grace, God's Election and Decree.

4. *Barth's christological critique of Luther.*

a. *The Secret Will of God—Divine Decision apart from the Election of Jesus Christ.*

As Barth makes his christological critique of the history of the doctrine of Election he is confronted with Luther's dualistic view of God, both in reference to God's Will or divine decision, in reference to the Being of God Himself and to the destiny of men. Barth states that long before Calvin, Luther spoke of a divine decision which took place apart from Christ, a decision hidden and unsearchable but not on that account any the less real. In other words, in this hidden and unsearchable but nevertheless real decision Luther had found the true and ultimate reality of the divine Election. Luther therefore does not according to Barth have a christological understanding of the Divine Decree. However, Barth is aware that there is a difference between the young Luther and the older Luther in this regard. The older Luther made the christological reference the only thing that mattered. Yet the older Luther ranked the *De Servo Arbitrio* (1525) as one of his best works. Thus there had not been any theoretical abandonment of the earlier position.[52]

Brunner states that before 1525 Luther took the wrath of God so seriously that he accepted a double decree and denied that God willed that all should be saved. This is the Luther of *The Bondage of the Will.* Subsequently Luther taught that God wills that all should be saved and that non-acceptance is man's fault and in no way related to the decree of God. This change, suggests Brunner, grows out of the realization that the double decree was speculation based upon the scholastic distinction between the *voluntas signi* and the *voluntas beneplaciti.* The latter Luther finally equated with unsearchable Election as rejection and saw that it involved disputation concerning the *nuda divinitas* (naked Divinity), which one should flee like the devil himself. God wants one to look at the Word of God, which is equivalent to Jesus Christ and his grace.[53]

Luther discovered, according to Brunner, not only that one ought not to speculate on the hidden God, but that if one looks at Revelation one will discover that the inmost being of God, God's being Himself, is identical with God's being for man. According to Brunner, Luther did not rework his theological statements in line with this new discovery.[54]

Yet, Barth asks how can there be any confident turning to the *Deus incarnatus,* when behind Him and above Him another and different *voluntas maiestatis* is always laid down and maintained? Luther has not cleared up the question of the nature and content of this *voluntas maiestatis;* he has only rejected and suppressed it.[55]

b. *The Hidden and Revealed God.*

Barth sees that even though Luther warned against inquiring into the secret will of God, yet the establishment of such a secret will means that the revelation of God is only a relative truth about God. Barth fears that the question of the hidden God will emerge one day as the question of the true God. The reference to Jesus Christ in Election is artificial when it is accompanied by the assertion of a quite different *voluntas maiestatis.*[56]

All of this leads Luther to posit a dualism with respect to God's Being: the naked God, God in Himself and God clothed in His Word:

> Now, God in His own nature and majesty is to be left alone, in this regard, we have nothing to do with Him, nor does He wish us to deal with Him. We have to do with Him as clothed and displayed beauty, in which the Psalmist proclaims Him to be clothed (cf. Ps. 21.5). I say that the righteous God does not deplore the death of His people which He Himself works in them, but He deplores the death which He finds in His people and desires to remove from them. God preached works to the end that sin and death may be taken away, and we may be saved. 'He sent His word and healed them.' (Ps. 107.20). But God hidden in majesty neither deplores nor takes away death, but works life, and death, and all in all, nor has He set bounds to Himself by His Word but has kept Himself free over all things.[57]

Luther insists that we may not debate the secret will of Divine Majesty and that any man is reckless who attempts to search out the secrets of Divine Majesty; for man cannot attain unto them since they dwell in inaccessible light. Luther quotes St. Paul in I Timothy 6:16. This text speaks of God Himself as dwelling in the light which no man can approach. Luther uses this text then as a basis for a distinction between the Hidden and Revealed God, between the secret will and the revealed will of God, for he goes on to say: "But let man occupy himself with God Incarnate, that is with Jesus crucified, in whom as Paul says (Cf. Col. 2.3) are all the treasures of wisdom and knowledge (though hidden.)." [58]

c. *Luther's view of Reprobation.*

As Luther spoke of a dualism in the will of God and a dualism in the Being of God, so this leads to a dualism in the destiny of men. Luther says that it belongs to the same God Incarnate to weep, lament, and groan over the perdition of the ungodly, though that will of majesty purposely leaves and reprobates some to perish.[59]

Barth attributes to Luther the view of Double Predestination. He interprets Luther as holding to the view that Predestination means quite unequivocally Double Predestination: double in the sense that Election and rejection are now two species within the one genus designated by the term Predestination. This was the view not only of Luther but also of the Reformers, of Zwingli, of Calvin.[60]

As Thomas Aquinas spoke of man's free choice which led to Reprobation, so Luther also espoused a subjective Election which was intimately and inseparably connected with Faith and Justification.[61]

In the final analysis Luther, according to Barth, did not have a sufficiently christological view of the divine decree, of the Being of God and of the destiny of man, of Election and Reprobation. Luther did not wholly identify Jesus Christ with the Electing God and he did not wholly identify the will of God with the divine decree of salvation.

5. *Barth's christological critique of Calvin.*

a. *Calvin's concept of a secret decree of God.*

In general Barth's objection to Calvin and Calvinism is the same as that directed to Luther. Barth finds that in Calvinism Jesus Christ is not really the Electing God, not the Election itself, not our Election, but only an elected means whereby the Electing God-electing elsewhere and in some other way—executes that which He had decreed concerning those whom He has elsewhere and in some other way—elected. Calvin does not equate the *Deus revelatus* with the *Deus absconditus.* Therefore all the dubious features of Calvin's doctrine result from the basic failing, that in the last analysis he separates God and Jesus Christ, thinking that what was in the beginning with God must be sought elsewhere than in Jesus Christ.[62]

The heart of Calvin's secret decree of God is his concept of the Double Predestination. Barth says that it is true that not only in Luther but in Calvin too there are passages in which the matter is expounded with the same disproportion, the same over-emphasis upon the positively evangelical element, as had obviously appeared necessary to Thomas. Yet of Calvin it must be said that at any rate in his stricter teaching he did not think it possible to dispense with this fatal parallelism of the concepts Election and Rejection.[63]

Calvin himself defines Predestination as the eternal decree of God in this double parallelism of Election and rejection:

> Predestination we call the eternal decree of God, by which he has determined in himself, what he would have to become of every individual of mankind. For they are not all created with a similar destiny; but eternal life foreordained for some, and eternal damnation for others. Every man, therefore, being created for one or the other of these ends, we say, he is predestinated either to life or to death.[64]

Calvin therefore goes beyond Aquinas and Luther in the matter of Reprobation. Thomas gave men a free choice to reject God and thus for this reason to be reprobated. Luther held to Faith and Justification. Calvin held to an extreme Double Predestination related to the secret counsel of God.[65]

Thus, according to Calvin's system, God is Himself the cause of the Fall of Adam into sin and the cause of Reprobation as Calvin writes:

> I confess, indeed, that all the descendants of Adam fell by the Divine will into that miserable condition in which they are now involved, and this is what I asserted from the beginning, that we must always return at last to the sovereign determination of God's Will, the cause of which is hidden in himself.[66]

Calvin teaches further that Predestination causes men to reject the Gospel.[67] God is the cause of unbelief according to Calvin.[68] God is also the cause of the Fall of Adam.[69]

Loraine Boettner and Emil Brunner both concur in the judgment that Calvin taught that both the Election of the saved and the Reprobation of the lost are connected with the eternal purpose of God.[70] Brunner says that if the accomplishment of man's salvation is based upon an eternal Decree, then the accomplishment of man's destruction is also based upon a divine decree in Calvinism.[71]

Whereas in Barth God's Yes is His last Word, in Calvin the Yes and No of God are equal words and therefore there is a twofold word in the counsel of God and in the Gospel.

b. *Calvin's christological security.*

Yet, Calvin points to Jesus Christ as the basis of the assurance of our Election as Luther did before him. We find no assurance of our Election in ourselves, not even in God the Father, considered alone, abstractedly from the Son. Christ therefore is the mirror in which it behoves us to contemplate our Election, and here we may do it with safety says Calvin.[72] The confidence of our salvation is rooted in Christ, and rests on the promises of the Gospel.[73] Calvin directs us away from the secret counsel of God and points us to Jesus Christ as the mirror of our Election.[74] Christ manifests to us our Election.[75]

But Barth is not satisfied with this because it fails to wholly identify Christ with the Divine Decree of God which tells us of Grace as the beginning of all the works and ways of God and as God's last Word.

6. *Barth's christological critique of Later Reformed Theology, Seventeenth Century Lutheran Orthodoxy and Federal Theology.*

a. *The Absolute Decree of Reformed Theology.*

The Calvinists or Reformed Theologians of Orthodoxy in the seventeenth century emphasized the Secret Counsel of God or the absolute decree of Predestination. Barth sides with the Reformed party in its struggle against the Remonstrants and Lutherans to safeguard the tenet that that which motivates the will of God is not to be sought outside of God Himself, but solely in His free good-pleasure. It is not to be sought in a created reality foreseen by God, nor is it to be sought in the good will of man, or the use which he makes of divine grace, or the meritorious work of faith, or even faith itself, or prayer or perseverance, or the dignity and worth of the race. Nor is it to be sought even in the *meritum Christi:* the obedience as such which was rendered by the man Jesus. All that is an effect and result of the divine Election, but not its basis. The Election itself is Grace, free Grace, having its origin and basis in God alone and not elsewhere.[76]

b. *The Supralapsarian-Infralapsarian Controversy within the Reformed Faith.*

The Supralapsarian-Infralapsarian controversy concerned itself with the object of God's decree of Predestination: is it man before his Creation or man after the Fall into sin.[77] According to the Supralapsarian system the original and proper purpose of God consists quite simply in this: that God Himself, and His glory, and more particularly His mercy and justice, should be revealed among men and to men by means of the salvation of some and the damnation of others. To this proper divine will and decree of God everything else that God wills is subordinate. As an interrelated means to its accomplishment, God has decreed that man should be created in such a way that by his own fault but with unfailing certainty he should fall into sin, thus arriving at the status and situation which would be a means to reveal the mercy of God in the salvation of some men and the justice of God in the damnation of others.[78]

The Supralapsarian views the Creation and the Fall as part of God's plan and purpose, as necessary to God's basic will: the Election of some men and the Reprobation of others. For the sake of His own glory God from all eternity predestinated each individual man either to the one alternative or to the other, either to Election or to Reprobation.[79] The *obiectum praedestinationis* is, then, man as he is seen by God in His eternal Election, i.e. *homo creabilis et labilis*.[80]

The Infralapsarian also knows of a primal and basic plan of God. For him, too, God's eternal purpose is to reveal and to glorify Himself. Creation and evil are part of God's plan by the efficient will of God in the case of Creation, and by God's permissive will in the case of Evil. The Fall is inevitable because it is an event decreed by God. Unlike the Supralapsarian, however, the Infralapsarian, does not think that he has any exact knowledge either of the content of God's primal and basic plan or of the reasons for the divine decree in respect of Creation and the Fall. The reasons for this decree are ultimately unknown and unknowable. Creation and the Fall were not absolutely necessary in order for God to reveal the divine mercy and justice.[81]

According to the Infralapsarian system the decree of Predestination is subordinated to the decree of Creation and the Fall which has its basis elsewhere. Only in the decree of Predestination as such does he come across the particular divine purpose to reveal God's mercy and justice by the salvation of some and the damnation of others. But the existence of sin and the existence of man as a sinner, and his existence at all, cannot be explained by that purpose.[82]

Predestination according to the Infralapsarian system has to do with a being which has already been raised from non-being to being. It has to do with an already existent being, and with a specific form of the existence of this being.[83] Man is the object of the eternal Predestination precisely in the situation in which God knows him as the one whom He will encounter in time.[84] And that means that God's choice between men was made not according to a physical predetermination but according to an ethical judgment. He made that choice from all eternity, but with reference to man as already created and fallen.[85]

c. *Barth's christological evaluation of the Supralapsarian-Infralapsarian controversy.*

Barth's judgment is that the doctrine of Predestination as taught both by Supralapsarianism and Infralapsarianism does not proclaim the free Grace of God as glad tidings, but as the neutral importation of the message that from all eternity God is gracious to whom He will be gracious, and when He will He hardeneth, and that this constitutes the limit within which each individual must run his course. The Supralapsarian maintains that this system of the eternal Election as Reprobation of individuals is the system above every other system being identical with the primal and basic plan of God besides which there is none other. The Infralapsarian allows the existence of another plan or system either alongside or prior to it in the form of the decree of Creation and the Fall. But both parties presuppose and maintain that that system is in any case from all eternity and that it is indeed fixed and unalterable, so that not merely individuals, but God Himself is its eternal author and is bound by it in time, and there can be nothing new under the sun, whether on man's part or on God's.[86]

Barth contends that behind these views of Supra and Infralapsarianism there stands the picture of the absolute God in Himself who is neither conditioned nor self-conditioning, and not the picture of the Son of God who is self-conditioned and therefore conditioned in His union with the Son of David; not the picture of God in Jesus Christ.[87]

d. *The Dutch Remonstrants and the Decretum Absolutum.*

At the end of the sixteenth and beginning of the seventeenth centuries there arose a lively opposition to the Calvinistic doctrine of the *decretum absolutum.*[88] On the one hand, there was the opposition within the Reformed Church itself. This was mainly the Dutch Remonstrants named after Jacob Arminius.[89]

The basis of Election according to this system was man himself. In the understanding of God and His relationship with man, the criterion or measure of all things was man, that is, man's conception of that which is right and rational and worthy of God and man. It was in the light of this basic doctrine of the absolute decree the assertion that we cannot and must not state that God elects and rejects whom He wills solely on the basis of His own free will or good-pleasure and without reference to conduct, and particularly to belief or unbelief, obedience or disobedience. On the contrary, the divine Election is made with due consideration of the conduct of men as foreseen by God from all eternity, i.e., of the use which, according to God's foreknowledge, they make of their freedom, whether in belief or unbelief, whether in obedience or disobedience.[90]

Barth must also reject this system and reject it entirely because not only did the Remonstrants not say that Christ is the Electing God, but they also said that there is no divine decision at all. There is only the establishment of a just and reasonable order of salvation of which Christ must be regarded as the content and the decisive instrument. Above and beyond that, there is no more than a divine foreknowledge of what individuals will become as measured by the order of salvation and on the basis of the use which they make of their creaturely freedom.[91]

According to the system of the Remonstrants there is no Electing God and no divine decree and salvation is not the result of a divine Election and Christ is not the Electing God, nor is He the content of the divine decree of Election from all eternity. This system is further away from Barth's than is Calvin's absolute decree.

e. *Barth's rejection of Federal Theology.*

During the seventeenth century there was another theology to be found in the Reformed Faith in which the concept of the covenant played so decisive a role that it came to be known as the Federal Theology. It is usually connected with the name of John Coçcejus.[92]

1. *A limited group of the elect.*

This system teaches that first there came the covenant of works. But this was abrogated by sin. A new covenant is put into its place. The covenant of Grace is from all eternity and in its temporal fulfilment a kind of separate arrangement is made between God and particular men, the elect, which means in practice the true adherents of the true Israelitish-Christian religion. A theology of biblical history was now replaced by a theology of biblical histories. In the recognition of the covenant the atonement made in Jesus Christ was no longer accepted as the revelation of it.[93]

In these histories we see examples in which certain men as distinct from others emerge as genuine hearers of the Word of God and partners in His work. They, and others like them, must obviously be regarded as the covenant-partners of God, and only they. In this way the conception of the covenant led into a blind alley in which it could not embrace and apply to all but only to some: Those who could be regarded as the elect in virtue of their personal relationship with God as determined one way or another—as though this is not necessarily contradicted by the calling and attitude of all genuine hearers of the Word of God and partners in His work, as though in relation to the God active and revealed in Jesus Christ we cannot, and must not, see that all other men are under the sign of the covenant set up by Him, so that far from any particularism we have to look on them with hope. Thus if we do not look exclusively to Jesus Christ and therefore to God we lose the capacity on this basis to think inclusively says Barth.[94]

2. *The Pact between the Father and the Son.*

The Federal Theology projects the unfolding of a pre-temporal occurrence, an eternal and free contract or pact made between God the Father and God the Son, in which the Father represents the righteousness and the Son the mercy of God, the latter adopting the function of a Mediator and pledge in the place of men.[95]

Barth maintains that with the conclusion of this contract with Himself that He ceases to be a righteous God in *abstracto* and becomes the God who in His righteousness is also merciful and therefore able to exercise grace. In this case it is not impossible or illegitimate to believe that properly, in some inner depth of His being behind the covenant of Grace, He might not be able to do this.[96]

3. *False View of the Trinity, Dualism in God, uncertainty about the Will of God.*

Barth here introduces some questions about the view of the Trinity in Federal Theology. He asks whether we can really think of the first and second persons of the triune Godhead as two divine subjects and therefore as two legal subjects who can have dealings and enter into obligations one with another. Barth regards this as mythology for which there is no place in a right understanding of the doctrine of the Trinity as the doctrine of the three modes of being of the one God, which is how it was understood and presented in Reformed orthodoxy. Barth maintains that God is one God, that He is one subject. We cannot therefore regard the divine persons of the Father and the Son as partners in this contract, but they are God-Father, Son and Holy Spirit—as the one partner, and the reality of man as distinct from God as the other.

When the covenant of Grace was based on a pact between two divine persons, a wider dualism was introduced into the Godhead—again in defiance of the Gospel as the revelation of the Father by the Son and of the Son by the Father, which took place in Jesus Christ. The result, according to Barth, was an uncertainty which necessarily relativized the unconditional validity of the covenant of Grace, making it doubtful whether in the relevation of this covenant we really had to do with the one will of the one God. If in God there are not merely different and fundamentally contradictory qualities, but also different subjects, who are indeed united in this matter, but had first of all to come to an agreement, how can the will of God seen in the history of the covenant of Grace be known to be binding and unequivocal, the first and final Word of God? The way is then opened up on this side too for considering the possibility of some other form of His will. The question is necessarily and seriously raised of a will of God the Father which originally and basically is different from the will of God the Son.[97]

Barth's own view of the triune Godhead coincides with his view of Jesus Christ as the electing God.

4. *God's Covenant Partner in Eternity.*

Barth's peculiar and particular view of the pre-existence of the God-Man Jesus Christ is introduced here as a refutation of the pact or contract concept of Federal Theology. Barth says that in this free act of the Election of Grace the Son of the Father is no longer just the eternal Logos but as such, as very God from all eternity He is also the very God and very man He will become in time. In the divine act of predestination there preexists the Jesus Christ who as the Son of the eternal Father and the child of the Virgin Mary will become and be the Mediator of the Covenant between God and man, the One who accomplishes the act of atonement. Jesus Christ is He in whom the covenant of Grace is fulfilled and revealed in history and is also its eternal basis. He who in Scripture is attested to be very God and very man is also the eternal pact between God and man.[98]

The covenant in Federal Theology is not identified with Jesus Christ but is an agreement between God the Father and God the Son. All the uncertainties of Calvin's absolute decree creep back into this system according to Barth.

f. *Seventeenth Century Lutheran Orthodoxy.*

1. *The Universal Loving-Kindness of God.*

Lutheran Orthodoxy spoke of a doctrine known as "De universali Dei misericordia et beneficia erga omnes voluntate" (Gerhard, Quenstedt). There is a *catholicismus paternal miserationis.* Its subject is God the Father. Its object is the whole of fallen humanity. Its basis within the Godhead is the *interventio Filii Dei.* The general loving kindness of God toward all men instead of the Election in eternity is the basis of salvation in Lutheranism.[99]

2. *Christology.*

There is a will of God concerning the salvation of all men. God, however, elects whom He elects in view of the two-fold fact present to His foreknowledge from all eternity: the fact of the work of Christ and the fact of faith directed towards that work. Barth recognizes that Election does play a part in the Lutheran system. God's eternal will to save all men is directed to those who are called to faith in Jesus Christ and who are obedient to this calling. To that extent Barth says it is an electing will.[100]

Yet, Barth questions whether we can take this fact at its face value. Is it really a question of Jesus Christ and not rather of the divine *benevolentia* as such understood as a systematic principle? Barth rejects the judicial character of the self-offering of the Son of God in Lutheran Orthodoxy.[101]

Barth rejects the Lutheran solution because it places a systematic principle in the place of Jesus Christ as a Person in the matter of salvation and Election. There must not be any systematization or setting up of a principle which binds God in advance and thus anticipates and secretly controls the reality. Barth says that the Gospel is the one thing which does not lend itself to be translated as transformed into such a principle. For the Gospel is what it is in the divine-human person of Jesus Christ Himself. And this person does not permit Himself to be translated into a proposition. It is not our task to understand this person in the light of a Gospel abstractly formulated and presupposed. Our task, says Barth, is to understand the concrete Gospel in the light of the person.[102]

Lutheranism has substituted for the absolute Decree of Calvin and Calvinism a universal love of God (*catholicismus paternae miserationis*). In Lutheran teaching the fact that God elects can mean no more and no less than that God wills and affirms in advance that which He knows will take place within the sphere of His ordained redemptive will. But this is not a free electing on the part of God. God ordains that those who in faith embrace the *meritum Christi* will be saved. In place, then, of a true Election there is instead an Election of an order of salvation dependent upon the work of Christ and the faith of men.[103]

Here is Barth's christological judgment of election systems that either set up an absolute decree or some kind of redemptive order such as we find in the Orthodox systems of Calvinism and Lutheranism in the seventeenth century:

> Thus when we think of the origin of grace and the beginning of all things, we cannot and must not think either of divine caprice or divine loving kindness, for these are both general and therefore without real content. What we must think of is Jesus Christ.[104]

Chapter III

EXPOSITION OF BARTH'S POSITION THAT JESUS CHRIST IS THE ELECTING GOD AND ELECT MAN

Jesus Christ Is Concrete Deity

1. *Barth's Definition of the Trinity.*

We have seen Barth analyzing the history of the doctrine of Election and rejecting the various traditional systems because of their failure to identify Jesus Christ with the electing God and the Decree of God. Actually we cannot really isolate these three christological aspects of Barth's doctrine of Election. The Electing God is the Elect Man and the Elect Man is the Electing God. The Decree is the decision which the Electing God made concerning Himself as the Elect Man. For this reason we have to look at Barth's concept of God and of the Trinity. For Barth the Electing God and Elect Man are not unknown quantities but are known. They have to do with only one name and with the same person, Jesus Christ.[105]

Barth will have nothing to do with an abstract God. God must be christologically defined. In Jesus Christ the Electing God, the Elect Man and the divine Decree are one. God is not one who in His deity exists only separated from man. In Jesus Christ there is no isolation of man from God or of God from man, in Him we encounter the history, the dialogue, in which God and man meet together and are together, the reality of the covenant mutually contracted, and fulfilled by them. Jesus Christ is in His one Person, as true God, man's loyal partner, and as true man, God's.[106]

But it is not only in time but already in eternity that the Electing God is the true God. If Jesus Christ is the

Electing God how then does Barth understand the traditional doctrine of the Trinity? Barth clearly rejects the idea of "persons" as implying that in God there are three different personalities or three self-existent individuals with their own special self-consciousness, cognition, volition, activity, effects, revelation and name. Barth prefers to speak of the one name of the one God, of the one personality of God. The one active and speaking divine Ego is the Father, Son and Holy Spirit. There are not three Subjects in God, but only one. The Trinity means that in the one God there is self-repetition, in the repetition of His own and equal divine being. Barth speaks of the three different modes of being and that this was the original meaning of the term "person." God does not exist as such outside or behind or above these modes of being. He does not exist otherwise than as Father, Son and Holy Spirit.[107]

The Trinity is the concrete Deity as opposed to all other concepts of God which are abstract as contained in heathen religions and mythologies and philosophies. The true and living God is the One whose Godhead consists in this history, who in these three modes of being is the One God, the Eternal, the Almighty, the Holy, the merciful, the One who loves in His freedom and is free in His love.[108]

The question arises as to whether Barth has given up the traditional understanding of the doctrine of the Trinity in order to support his concept of Jesus Christ as the Electing God. Does Barth teach the old heresy of Modalism and Patripassianism (that the Father suffers also)? Hamer states that Barth shows in his theology that Election is above all a decision which touches God Himself, a divine decision which brings God to manifest Himself externally in His Word. This point is intimately connected with Barth's teaching on the Trinity. There is not a real Trinity of persons, not three really distinct hypostases. Barth's solution is unwittingly one of modalities. The Logos is God as He speaks, revealing Himself, God as he goes out of Himself, appearing in a new light.[109]

Barth's view of God and the Trinity could be described as christological monotheism.

2. *Relationship of Jesus Christ to the Trinity.*

Against the background of Barth's concept of three

modes of being in God as the meaning of the Trinity we consider next the relationship of Jesus Christ to the Trinity. Barth does not merely speak of the Son of God as pre-existing before the Incarnation which is the traditional way of speaking but Barth actually speaks of Jesus Christ as in the beginning with God. He does not regard Jesus Christ as primarily an historical phenomenon. According to Barth Jesus Christ did not exist in the beginning with God in the sense that all things may be said to have been in the beginning with God according to His eternal knowing and willing. The Son of God is one with the Son of Man as foreordained from all eternity. Jesus Christ was in the beginning with God in the sense that all Creation and its history was in God's plan and decree. This further means that Jesus Christ is Himself the plan and decree of God, Himself the divine decision with respect to all Creation and its history whose content is already determined.[110].

Barth then cannot be accused as teaching that Jesus was already the Incarnate One, already born of the Virgin Mary in eternity as when He was on earth. Jesus Christ was the Incarnate One in eternity in the sense of God's intention, will and decree. This is in harmony with Scripture which teaches that Christ was the Lamb of God slain from the foundation of the world and yet it was not until Calvary that the Lamb of God was actually slain (I Peter 1:18-20).

As the subject and object of this choice, this decision or decree, Jesus Christ was at the beginning. This is not the beginning of God, for God has indeed no beginning. But He was at the beginning of all things, at the beginning of God's dealings with the reality which is distinct from Himself. Jesus Christ was the choice of Election of God in respect of this reality. He was the Election of God's Grace as directed towards man.[111]

This means that Jesus Christ is not only the decision of God in eternity but also its manifestation in time. Here we see another aspect of the relationship of Jesus Christ to the Trinity. From all eternity God willed to become man in Jesus Christ for our good, did become man in time for our good, and will be and remain man in eternity for our good.[112]

Barth relates the modality of the Trinitarian life of God to the Incarnation. The modality of the Trinitarian life of God means that in the Incarnation God becomes what He had not previously been. He takes into unity with His divine being a quite different, a creaturely and indeed a sinful being. God empties Himself, He humbles Himself. But He does not do it apart from its basis in His own being, in His own inner life. He does not do it without any correspondent to, but as the strangely logical final continuation of, the history in which He is God. God does not need to deny, abandon and leave behind or even diminish His Godhead to do this. He does not need to leave the work of the Reconciler in the doubtful hands of a creature. He can enter in Himself, seeing He is in Himself not only the One who rules and commands in majesty, but also in His own divine person, although in a different mode of being, the One who is obedient in humility.[113]

Thus even the doctrine of the Trinity is interpreted christologically by Barth.

The Concrete Decree

1. *Jesus Christ is the Electing God.*

On this basis of the modality of God's Being Barth contends that Jesus Christ is the Electing God, the subject of Election. The Electing God is the meaning of the trinitarian life of God. There is no question of rivalry between the Father and the Son because the Father and the Son are one in this unity of the divine name and glory. The Son, then, is an active Subject of the *aeterna Dei praedestinatio* as Son of Man, that He is Himself the Electing God, and that only in this way and therefore in an unlimited divine sovereignty, is He the Elect, the One who is subjected to the divine Predestination, the Son who is voluntarily obedient to the Father; that only in this way and for this reason is He the Son of Man establishing and fulfilling the will of God in the world.[114]

This means, according to Barth, that we cannot go beyond the Electing God who is Jesus Christ. We must not ask concerning any other but Him. In no depth of the Godhead shall we encounter any other but Him. There is no such thing as Godhead in itself. Godhead is always the Godhead of the Father, the Son and the Holy Spirit. He tells us that Himself is the One who elects us.[115]

2. *Jesus Christ is the Elect Man.*

Jesus Christ is not only the Electing God but also the Elect Man, not only the subject of Election but also the object of Election. Jesus Christ is not merely one of the Elect as was the christological assertion of tradition in the Church.[116] It was in virtue of His divinity that He was ordained and appointed Lord and Head of all others, the organ and instrument of the whole Election of God and the revelation and reflection of the Election of those who were elected with Him.

Jesus Christ is the object of God's pre-temporal, eternal divine decision. It is in and with the existence of this man that the eternal divine decision has as its object and content the execution of the divine covenant with man, the salvation of all men. Man is the object of the eternal decision and foreordination. Jesus Christ is not merely one of the elect but the Elect of God. From the beginning, from eternity itself as elected Man Jesus Christ does not stand alongside the rest of the elect, but before and above them as the One who is originally and properly the Elect. There are no other elect together or apart from Him. Barth finds support for this in Ephesians 1:4 which says, only "in" Him. "In Him," according to Barth's interpretation, does not simply mean with Him, together with Him, in His company. Nor does it mean only through Him, by means of that which He as elected man can be and do for them. "In Him" means in His person, in His will, in His own divine choice, in the basic decision of God which He fulfills over against every man.[117]

God decreed that this Man should be the cause and the instrument of our exaltation.[118] Barth can speak of Jesus Christ as both the Elect and as the cause of our Election. The object of Election is christologically reinterpreted by Barth.

But even as the object of Predestination, even as elected man, Jesus Christ must still be understood as truly the beginning of all God's ways and works.[119]

Barth interprets man christologically and thus man is elect man. Man is that being who is elected in Jesus Christ. Thus we have a christological anthropology in Barth.

3. *Jesus Christ is the Decree of God.*

There is no will of God, no covenant between God the Father and God the Son, no covenant between God and man, no absolute decree above or beyond Jesus Christ. Jesus Christ is the Election itself. Barth goes so far as to say that there is no will or covenant apart from Jesus Christ. The covenant or decree of God is christologically defined. Barth maintains that in Jesus Christ we do not have to do with a second, and subsequent, but with the first and original content of the will of God, before and above which there is no other will, either hidden or revealed in some other way, in the light of which we might have to understand and fear and love God and interpret man very differently from how they are both represented in Jesus Christ. We do not need to look beyond Jesus Christ. When we look at Him we have all conceivable clarity.[120]

Jesus Christ is therefore the First Word of God, the Grace and Atonement of God. For this reason Barth puts the Gospel before the Law. In the Lutheran tradition the Law comes before the Gospel. Barth sees first the Gospel, the gracious claim of God. Jesus Christ is the unity of the Gospel and the Law. He is the promise and the command. He is the Gospel and the Law, the address of God to man and the claim of God upon man.[121] Barth interprets the relationship between the Law and the Gospel christologically. Law is not God's first word nor is it the last Word. Gospel is both first and last Word.

The decree of God which is Jesus Christ is therefore also a double decree but unlike Calvinism which teaches a double decree directed toward the destiny of men it is a decree directed at God and man. In Jesus Christ God in His free Grace determines Himself for sinful man and sinful man for Himself. God takes upon Himself the rejection of man with all the consequences, and elects man to participation in His own glory.[122] This is the concrete decree of God in contrast to the absolute decree of Calvinism.[123]

In this double decree man stands to gain while God stands only to lose. This eternal divine Predestination is identical with the Election of Jesus Christ. Its twofold content is that God wills to lose in order that man may gain. There is a sure and certain salvation for man, and a sure and certain risk for God.[124]

Again we see another christological turn of events in the thought of Karl Barth on Election. The decree of God, salvation and damnation are christologically defined.

Chapter IV

THE REJECTION OF JESUS CHRIST AND THE REJECTION OF INDIVIDUAL MEN: BARTH'S VARIOUS SOLUTIONS TO THE PROBLEM OF REJECTION, DAMNATION AND REPROBATION

Jesus Christ as the Only Man Rejected By God

1. *Barth's understanding of "Double Predestination."* Already in his "Epistle to the Romans," long before he wrote his now famous "Church Dogmatics," Barth had reinterpreted the Augustinian-Calvinistic understanding of the traditional doctrine of Double Predestination. He speaks of it in *the Epistle to the Romans* as an eternal two-sided possibility which confronts all men; which moves and rests in God alone—the roots of their existence are deeply buried in the unity of God.[125] The doctrine does not mean that a certain human being or having or doing is as such approved and some other human behaviour is as such rejected. Nor that some are able to comfort themselves in the temporal enjoyment of eternal Election while others are in possession of a temporal knowledge of their eternal rejection. In *the Epistle to the Romans* Barth took the position that the contest between Election and rejection is paradoxical.[126]

Barth regards the Reformers' use of the doctrine of Election and rejection as mythology. They applied this doctrine of Double Predestination to the psychological unity of this or that individual and they referred quantitatively to the elect and the damned. It was Barth's view that Paul did not think either quantitatively or psychologically. Paul dealt with God's concern for the individual and not with the individual's concern with God. Barth makes an ontological judgment when he asks how indeed can the temporal, observable, psychologically visible individual be at all capable of eternal Election or rejection? Barth speaks of the eternal victory of Election over rejection, of love over hate, of life over death.[127]

In *the Epistle to the Romans* Barth found the key in the concept of the freedom of God. The Election of the one and the rejection of the other have meaning only in the freedom of God. Rejection is subordinate to Election. The purpose of the rejection of Pharaoh is identical with that of the Election of Moses.[128] Election is defined in *the Epistle to Romans* by Barth as meaning the possible, though utterly incomprehensible salvation of men from the inevitable destiny of rejection. The "Yes" of God consists only in the transformation of His "No." [129]

When we come to the *Church Dogmatics* Barth sees God using His freedom in order to take upon Himself man's rejection. God has ascribed to Himself reprobation and perdition and to man salvation and life.[130] God has made Himself the object of the wrath and judgment to which man had brought himself; He took upon Himself the rejection which man had deserved; He tasted Himself the damnation, death and hell which ought to have been the portion of fallen man.[131] This is Barth's reinterpretation of the traditional doctrine of Double Predestination in Calvinism.

Predestination does have a negative side, it does contain a "No" but it is not a "No" spoken against man. Man is not rejected. Predestination does not speak of the rejection and death of man. This could have been the state of man. From all eternity God could have excluded man from this covenant but instead He elected man as a covenant-partner. In His Son He elected Himself as the covenant-partner of man.[132]

In the *Church Dogmatics* Barth proceeds to give Double Predestination a christological foundation and content. In Predestination we do not find a will of God directed equally towards man's life and man's death, towards his salvation and towards his damnation. God removed man's death and perdition and made it His own. That removing took place in Jesus Christ. It is in this fact that we see the eternal will of God.[133]

Barth admits that this interpretation of Double Predestination stands or falls with the view that the divine Predestination is to be understood only within the Election of Jesus Christ.[134]

2. *Rejection of Damnation christologically interpreted.*
a. *Who is rejected? Christ, not man.*

Already in *the Epistle to the Romans* there is a kind of christological Universalism. Barth regards Adam as the old subject, the ego of the man of this world. This Ego is fallen. This Fall is the condemnation unto death and is pronounced upon all men. This is the destiny of all men. But Christ is the new subject, the Ego of the coming world. This Ego receives and bears and reveals the divine Justification and Election.[135] Barth says that in the light of this act of obedience there is no man who is not in Christ. All are renewed and clothed with righteousness, all are become a new subject and are therefore set at liberty under the affirmation of God.[136]

In the *Church Dogmatics* Barth definitely speaks of Christ as the only rejected Man by God. He says that on the basis of this decree of God the only truly rejected man is His own Son, that God's rejection has taken its course and been fulfilled and reached its goal, with all that that involves, against the One, so that it can no longer fall on other men or be their concern. Men are still to be aware of the threat of their rejection, but it cannot now be their concern to suffer the execution of this threat, to suffer the eternal damnation which their godlessness deserves. The Son of God suffered in the place of the godless and so rejection can no longer be the concern or destiny of men or even their desire and undertaking. God has removed the merited rejection of man, and has laid it upon His own Son.[137] The decree of Election from eternity is the basis of this christological Universalism. In both *the Epistle to the Romans* and in the *Church Dogmatics* Barth looks to God in eternity, to the divine concrete decree of Election, to Jesus Christ the Man elected to bear the rejection of men and who is therefore the only rejected Man of God.

Barth is emphatic in stating that Christ is the only rejected One. Because Christ is the only rejected One and because He lived the life of One rejected such a life is objectively impossible for all others.[138]

When the question arises concerning those who reject what Jesus has secured for all, Barth affirms that it is an evil, perilous and futile misunderstanding and disregard of the fact that Jesus Christ alone is truly the rejected One of God.[139]

Jesus Christ is the rejected One because He is first the elected One. There is an identity then between Election and rejection in relation to Jesus Christ. On this basis Barth says that there is no other rejected but Himself. In His rejection He makes room for the others as the Elect of God. Barth affirms that Jesus Christ is the Lord and Head and Subject of the witness both of "the elect" and also of the "rejected." [140]

When the question is asked who is rejected, Barth answers: "Christ, not man."

b. *What is rejected: the Sin of man, Satan, the rejection of man is rejected.*

There is then according to Barth's doctrine of Election no Dualism which is eternal. There is no eternal covenant of wrath which corresponds on the one side to the eternal covenant of grace on the other.

What is rejected? The sin of man is rejected. Jesus as judged or rejected means the end of sin. We know that we are guilty of sin. But we are now no longer pledged or committed to it. There is no ground for evil now. The ground for evil has been cut from under our feet. It is only in unbelief that we think we can still have that freedom to live in sin.[141]

What is rejected? Satan and the demonic and evil are rejected. The Election of Jesus Christ and the Election of man the creature in Jesus Christ means the rejection of Satan, the rebel angel who is the very sum and substance of the possibility which is not chosen by God, the very essence of the creature in its misunderstanding and misuse of its Creation and destiny and in its desire to be as God, to be itself a god. Satan (and the whole kingdom of evil, i.e., the demonic, which has its basis in him) is the shadow which accompanied the light of the Election of Jesus Christ.

Man in himself and in his creaturely freedom has no power to reject that which in His divine freedom God rejects. Man in himself will always do as Adam did in Genesis 3. Man in himself incurs the rejection which rests upon his temptation and corruption. Exposed to the power of the divine negation and rejection, he is guilty of death. But it is this very man in himself and as such who in and with the Election of the man Jesus is loved of God from all eternity and elected to fellowship with Him. In this one Man Jesus God puts at the head and in the place of all other men the One who has the same power as Himself to reject Satan and to maintain and not surrender the goodness of man's divine Creation and destiny.[142]

The destiny of mankind is christologically determined because if He did not stand at their head, if they were not elected "in Him," without Him and outside of Him they would be forever rejected.[143]

What is rejected? The rejection of man is rejected. Even rejection itself, the rejection of man is rejected. Rejection must be christologically interpreted according to Barth.

Barth affirms that in Jesus Christ the rejected can only have been rejected in the sense that it is a matter of the past. Men cannot be rejected any more. Between man and an independent existence of his own as rejected there stands the death which Jesus Christ has suffered in his place, and the resurrection by which Jesus Christ has opened up for him His own place as elect. There is no future possibility on the part of man to decide against his election. His rejection has been taken away in Jesus Christ.[144]

Since Jesus Christ has borne eternally and therefore for all time the rejection of mankind, it is therefore the rejection which is "rejected." The rejected man is quite other than the elect. The rejected man is the man who is not willed by God. It is only as the object of the divine nonwilling that he exists as a rejected man.[145]

The reason why man is no longer rejected is because God Himself has suffered for the sinner. God is far greater than we, therefore His sorrow is so much greater than ours on our behalf than any sorrow which we can feel for ourselves. Because God is merciful the divine pain of sorrow is taken from us and forbidden to us. It would be something presumptuous to try to bear our sorrows—a tragic consciousness to which we may not pretend. This is now God's concern and God's burden. Our suffering for sin has not touched us and cannot touch us as it touches Him. God gave His only begotten Son in order to remove this sorrow.[146]

Barth identifies the Judgment of God with the crucifixion of Christ and calls this the Terror of Good Friday. All the other judgments of history, upon Israel, upon the world, upon mankind can only foreshadow or reflect this Judgment. The Crucifixion of Christ is the revelation of the wrath of God against all ungodliness and unrighteousness of men. Only as we look at this event can we truly say that human sin and sinful man have become the object of the divine anger.[147]

No man could bear the wrath of God. Only God Himself could bear the wrath of God. Only God's mercy was capable of bearing the pain to which the creature existing in opposition to Him is subject. At Golgotha we see the double proof of omnipotence in which God did not abate the demands of His righteousness but showed Himself equal to His own wrath, on the one hand by submitting to it and on the other by not being consumed by it.[148]

There is a christological basis for the wrath and Judgment of God. Judgment is christologically defined in Barth's doctrine of Election.

Election and Ontology

1. *Nothingness as a threat.*

Barth has the unusual approach in his theology of seeing a point of theology from various angles. There is an ontological framework in Barth's understanding of the relationship between Election and rejection.

Barth gives to Nothingness an ontological status. It is not nothing or non-existent. God is concerned with it, He strives against it and resists it. Nothingness "is." [149] God is concerned with man the creature who is threatened by Nothingness. Man is God's partner in the struggle against Nothingness.[150] Nothingness is evil because it is the negation of God's Grace. It is that which opposes God and the creature. It is what is impossible or intolerable. Whether in the form of sin, evil or death, it is inexplicable as a natural process or condition.[151]

Nothingness has ontological status because it is that

which God has not willed, which God has rejected or excluded by His decision.

2. *Christological Defeat of Nothingness.*

God separates Himself from Nothingness and in the face of it He asserts Himself and exerts His positive will. Thus Nothingness is brought into connection with Election. God elects and therefore rejects what He does not elect. God opposes what He does not will. He says Yes, and therefore He says No to that to which He has not said Yes.[152]

God identifies Himself with the creature in the face of the threat of Nothingness. God knows its advantage over the creature. Yet He is Lord over this threat against His creature. He has sworn fidelity to His threatened creature. He has Himself assumed the burden and trouble of confrontation with nothingness. And here is perhaps the greatest sentence in the whole of the *Church Dogmatics:* the key to the whole understanding of Barth's theology in general and his doctrine of Election in particular:

> He would rather let Himself be injured and humiliated in making the assault and repulse of nothingness His own concern than leave His creature alone in this affliction. He deploys all His majesty in the work of His deepest condescension. He intervenes in the struggle between nothingness and the creature as if He were not God but Himself a weak and threatened and vulnerable creature.[153]

For Barth there is a christological understanding of the threat of Nothingness. There is christological defeat of Nothingness. This is the "No" of God, the *opus alienum,* the strange work of God, the activity of God on the left hand. Nothingness could threaten the creature but it was impotent against the God who humbled Himself, and Himself became a creature, and exposed Himself to its power and resisted it. Nothingness could not master this victim. It could neither endure nor bear the presence of God in the flesh. The fulness of the grace which God showed to His creature by Himself becoming a threatened, even ruined and lost creature, was its undoing. Therefore Nothingness has no perpetuity. It ceases to be even a receding frontier and fleeting shadow. This is what happened to Nothingness in the death of Jesus Christ, in the justification and deliverance of sinful man in this death.[154]

Barth's concept of the christological defeat of Nothingness harmonizes with the thesis that Jesus Christ is the only Man rejected by God.

There has been criticism of Barth's concept of Nothingness, of *Das Nichtige,* of Barth's concept of Nothingness as the impossible possibility. John Hick in his work on the problem of Theodicy entitled *Evil And The God of Love* regards Barth's concept of Nothingness as an infringement of his ban upon speculative theorizing and as a naively mythological construction, which cannot withstand rational criticism.[155] Hick believes that Barth has gone beyond the data of Christian Faith and has become entangled in the dangers of philosophical construction.[156] He further points out that the particular speculation in which Barth indulges is mythological rather than rational, and that its anthropomorphic character is a liability if it is intended to be a contribution to the science of theology.[157]

Hick asks the question whether this peculiar negative occurrence "on God's left hand" is something that He intends and plans, or something that takes place by necessity which is independent of His intention? When it is said that evil comes to "be" as the object of God's wrath, rejection and denial, we have to ask whether its so coming to "be" is desired and planned by God, or something occurring by a necessity that is contrary to His wish? Hick answers that the question is not resolved, but only postponed, by invoking the image of the left hand and the related notion of willing-against.[158]

The conclusion to which Hick comes is that we should not be expected to adopt Barth's own distinctive account of the nature and origin of evil as a revealed truth which must be accepted in faith, for it does not represent revealed truth at all. Hick believes that it is only the product of Barth's own fertile and fascinating mind. The notion that evil has been brought into "existence" as that which God rejected when he elected His good creation, is not among the data of Christian faith.[159]

In answer to Hick's criticism of Barth's concept of the Nihil or Nothingness or the nature and origin of Evil I should like to point out the following:

a. The Bible itself does not give us a systematic account of the origin of evil. There are mythological and anthropomorphic expressions or elements in the Biblical account. In Genesis chapter 3 you have the story of the serpent and the temptation of Adam and Eve in the Garden of Eden. In the Book of Revelation in the New Testament, chapter 12 you have the account of war in Heaven and of the battle between Michael the archangel and the great Dragon and his angels and of Satan being cast out of Heaven. In the Book of Job you have Satan as the so called prosecuting attorney of Heaven. In the New Testament Satan is the adversary of God and man as we see in the account of the temptation of Jesus in the Wilderness (St. Matthew chapter 4). All of this points out that we have no systematic and rational account of evil in the Bible but evil presented in mythological and anthropomorphic pictures as that which God is opposed to. Barth's view should not therefore be criticized as mythological and anthropomorphic.

b. Barth has given us a christological interpretation of Nothingness and therefore a theological interpretation, one that seeks to be true to the Gospel and scriptural witness. Barth says that true nothingness is that which brought Jesus Christ to the cross, and that He defeated there. The Christ is the basis for our knowledge of Nothingness according to Barth. It is only from the standpoint of Jesus Christ, His birth, death and resurrection, do we see it in reality and truth. If there is confusion concerning Nothingness then it obviously is because we do not see it from the standpoint of Jesus Christ.[160]

Barth's christological interpretation reveals the concrete nature of Nothingness and its relation to the sin of man. He points out that in the light of Jesus Christ the concrete form in which Nothingness is active and revealed is the sin of man as his personal act and guilt, his aberration from the grace of God and its command, his refusal of the gratitude he owes to God, his arrogant attempt to be his own master. In the light of Jesus Christ it is impossible to escape the truth that we ourselves as sinners have become the victims and servants of nothingness, sharing its nature and producing and extending it.[161]

c. Barth does have scriptural basis for his concept of Nothingness. He turns to Genesis chapter three and states that the sin of man as depicted in Genesis three confirms the accuracy of his definition. It is purely and simply what God did not, does not and cannot will. Sin has the essence only of non-essence, and only as such can it exist. Yet the sin of man also confirms the real existence of Nothingness. Nothingness is a factor so real that the creature of God, and among His creatures man especially in whom the purpose of Creation is revealed, is not only confronted by it and becomes its victim, but makes himself its agent. And all the subsequent history of the relationship between God and His creature is marked by the fact that man is the sinner who has submitted and fallen a victim to chaos. The issue in this whole history is the repulse and final removal of the threat thus actualized. And God Himself is always the One who first takes this threat seriously, who faces and throws Himself against it, who strives with chaos, who persists in His attitude, who continues and completes the action which He has already undertaken as creator in this respect, negating and rejecting it.[162]

d. Barth's concept of Nothingness is consistent with the whole of his theology, with his understanding of the Gospel. If Barth's concept of Nothingness collapses then his whole understanding of the Gospel, his whole theological approach in his *Church Dogmatics* collapses. Barth's concept of the christological defeat of Nothingness and of the non-perpetuity of Evil is the main point of Barth's theological interpretation of Nothingness. Jesus is Victor is the theme of Barth's *Church Dogmatics*. Surely this is the theme of the Gospel of the New Testament.

e. In defense of Barth's concept of Nothingness Hartwell points out that Barth refers us to the freedom of God's will in which from all eternity He allowed the world and man to exist under the condition of sin, evil and death. God permits and tolerates the existence of the Nihil in order to safeguard man's autonomy and freedom in the interest of man's free response to His grace in Jesus Christ even though this involves the risk of man's falling away from Him. Above all, God's supreme and truest lovingkindness to His creature is said to be revealed in its full splendour only when the obedience and blessedness of man are not simply his nature but salvation from the edge of an abyss, when in his obedience and blessedness man is constantly reminded of his gracious Creation out of nothing and of his gracious preservation from the Nihil by the menacing proximity of realm of the Nihil, in short, when man's obedience and blessedness are the fruits of faith and thus of God's grace in Jesus Christ.[163]

Barth's concept of Nothingness preserves the Biblical relationship between God the Creator and man the creature, between Christ the Saviour and man the sinner.

The Freedom of God and Election

1. *Is there caprice in God?*

Although God is the Electing God, Barth speaks of the freedom of God as a possibility grounded in the being of God. There is no question of God Himself being controlled by caprice or chance. This freedom means that God can be lowly or exalted, abroad or at home, the One who is accused and judged as well as the Lord of Glory. The ability of God in His freedom to be the Reconciler of the world is not an arbitrary ability on the other hand. It is not, says Barth, a mere capacity to be now in this way and now in some other way, now above and now below. It is not a disorderliness and carelessness in God. God is not a victim driven to and fro by the dialectic of His divine nature, but is always His own master. He does not make just any use of the possibilities of His divine nature, but He makes one definite use which is necessary on the basis and in fulfilment of His own decision.[164]

The freedom of God in Barth's doctrine of Election is not the result of a necessary process internal or external to God which leads God to a certain inevitable goal such as the dialectical process in Hegel's philosophical system in which we see Being as the original thesis move out of itself to non-being as the antithesis and finally resulting in the synthesis of becoming. Hegel further speaks of Logic as the thesis opposed by Nature as the antithesis resulting in the synthesis known as Spirit. Spirit itself goes through the dialectical process as follows: Objective Spirit is the thesis, Subjective Spirit is the antithesis and Absolute Spirit is the higher synthesis. The synthesis is richer than the thesis. For Barth Grace is the beginning and end of all the ways and works of God. God's freedom does not contradict His love and Grace, His concrete decision for man, His Election of Jesus Christ. God is He who is free to love. God's freedom is His love and His love is His freedom. God is not the prisoner of His freedom or His love. He is His love, His freedom, His decision. Jesus Christ is the act of God's freedom, of His love, of His decision.

The decision of this freedom of God equally protects us from viewing God's freedom as an irrational, capricious, unstable, blind fate as we find in Schopenhauer's philosophical system of thought. We need not fear that God is different from Jesus Christ Who is the concrete decision of God, of the God who is free to love, that there is a God beyond Jesus Christ, a God whose secret will will contradict His concrete will in Jesus Christ. God's freedom is His freedom to be God for man; God has determined Himself for man.

The fulfilment of a divine decree takes place in the freedom of God. There is no possibility of something quite different happening. We are not dealing with one of the throws in a game of chance which takes place in the divine being, but with the foundation-rock of a divine decision which is as we find it divinely fulfilled in this saving event and not otherwise.[165]

2. *New decisions of the Predestinating God.*

Yet, this freedom of God which results in a divine decree also means that there are new decisions of the Predestinating God in Barth's doctrine of Election, God is free and remains free and He does not cease to make use of His freedom but continues to decide. Parallel to the course of God's eternal deciding we have constantly to reckon with new decisions in time. Barth looks to the Bible and says that there is no election which cannot be followed by rejection, no rejection which cannot be followed by election. God continues to be the Lord of all His works and ways. He is still consistent with Himself and with the prearranged order of election and rejection. But this means that He is always the living God. Barth does not deal with abstract systems or principles but with the Living God and the Person of Jesus Christ. God's life is dynamic. Thus there is a kind of dialectical movement in the history of Israel, the Church and the individual. God is free to love where He was wrath and to be wrath where He loved, to bring death to the living and life to the dead, to repent Himself and to repent of His repenting. This is Barth's understanding of how Predestination is described in the *locus classicus,* Romans 9-11, a description which we cannot possibly reconcile with the understanding of Predestination as a rigid and static law, but only with the understanding of it as a definition of God's eternal action in time.[166]

Parallel to God's eternal decision there is the question of the possibility for the unbeliever, the possibility of salvation for the fallen. This is the continuity of Barth's *Church Dogmatics* with his earlier *Epistle to the Romans.*[167]

Barth's concept of the freedom of God has led one critic to charge Barth with teaching in the final analysis an unknown God. This is the conclusion of Fred H. Klooster in his book: *The Significance of Barth's Theology;*

> There is a strange ambiguity in Barth's thought at this point—to say the least. It is interesting to notice that one of Barth's most basic objections to Calvin's doctrine of predestination is the charge that it involves an Unknown God. But this charge applies to Barth—not to Calvin. For Calvin the fact of God's sovereign election and reprobation are known, because God has clearly revealed this. But since God has not chosen to reveal the identity of the elect and reprobate, except in a rare instance as that of Jacob and Esau, we do not know the identity of the elect and reprobate. Yet by divine command, the gospel must be preached to all men, and through this means God will effectively bring his elect to salvation. Calvin also stresses that the man to whom God has given true faith may be assured of his eternal salvation as he looks into the mirror of Jesus Christ. However, Barth's view of election really seems to involve something of an Unknown God. Although all men are elect in Christ so that what Christ has done has been done for all men, Barth leaves open the question as to what the freedom of God might yet involve. Barth's leaving open the question of a possible universalism, and his refusal to affirm or deny this theory, seems to involve an unknown God. The frontier from election to rejection and vice versa can be repeatedly crossed

> and criss-crossed. In view of the freedom of God, Barth insists that we must leave open the possibility as to what will eventually happen. But this view of the freedom of God involves an Unknown God and is in conflict with Scripture.[168]

Klooster assumes that the Biblical narrative of the Election of Jacob and the rejection of Esau refers to the question of the ultimate destiny of Jacob and Esau, to their ultimate fate in eternity, salvation and damnation. Rowley in his work *The Biblical Doctrine of Election* points out the confusion in the relationship between Election and Damnation. Election in the Bible, according to Rowley is Election to service. The vessel of dishonor which the potter makes is still something that he wants, and that has a definite use. The metaphor of the potter can not be used to support the idea that God elects any to oppose Him. It implies that all the vessels, both those of honour and those of dishonour, are chosen, for all in their varying ways serve the potter's purpose, and the vessel that is destroyed is one for which the potter has no purpose or use. Whom God chooses, He chooses for service. There is variety of service, but it is all service, and it is all service for God. Whom God destroys, He finds no longer serviceable. Hence the use of this metaphor only supports the view that the Divine Election concerns exclusively the Divine service.[169]

The Biblical narrative concerning the Election of Jacob and the reprobation of Esau refers not to the ultimate destiny of their souls but to the economy of service in the time of the Patriarchs in the Old Testament.

It is not a question of a known and unknown God. It is a question of whether Calvin or Barth present the God witnessed to in the Scriptures. It is a question of a true concept of God versus a false concept of God. The known God of the calvinistic system is a God who already in eternity decreed the damnation of a certain number of people and decreed the salvation of a certain number of people. The known God of Barth's doctrine of Election is the God whose ways and works from beginning to end are the ways and works of grace, the God whose concrete decision and decree is Jesus Christ, the Man who is both elect and rejected.

Klooster fails to take note of the distinction between

the damnation of man and the damnation of Jesus Christ. Barth's pluralistic approach to the question of damnation has a scriptural basis. Man cannot ultimately experience what Jesus Christ has experienced in being rejected by God. There is the question of the possibility of damnation for men and its eschatological limit and finally there is the biblical proclamation of Christ's defeat of the forces of unbelief and evil. The known God of Barth's doctrine of Election is the triumph of God over evil. In other words Jesus is Victor. This is the God of Barth.

Barth's Distinction between the Man on the Left Hand and on the Right Hand and between the Flesh of Man and the Spirit of Men

1. *Man on the left and right hand of God.*

Another approach to this problem Barth sees in the distinction between the man on the left hand and the man on the right hand of God. The righteousness of God makes a separation which cuts man's existence at the very root, dividing him into a right and a left. On the left hand man determines himself as a doer of the wrong and thus is caught up in the divine judgment. On the right hand he does not cease to be a wrongdoer and therefore under the divine judgment, but determines himself as man, as the possession of God, in the kingdom of God, the object of His positive will and purpose, on the way to the goal which God has marked out for him. On the left hand he is the man who can only perish, who is overtaken by the wrath of God, who can only die, who has already been put to death and done away, and on the right hand he is the same man who even in this dying and perishing, even as the one who has been put away, is still the one who stands over against God, the object of His purposes, surrounded and maintained by His life.[170]

The concept of the man on the left hand and on the right hand of God harmonizes with the concept of Election as what God has not decreed and has decreed. God rejects the man on the left hand and accepts the man on the right. The man on the left hand is identical with the man on the right hand and helps us to understand Barth's thesis that Jesus Christ is the only man rejected by God.

2. *The christological Basis of the left hand and right hand of God.*

Barth maintains that he has not invented this concept of the left and right hand of God. He believes that there is a christological basis for it. This is all true and actual in Jesus Christ.[171] Jesus is both the Judge and the Judged; He is the subject and object in this history. He unites within Himself the antithesis of the man on the left hand and the man on the right hand of God. In this way He justifies sinful man.[172]

This means the victory of God's grace and right hand over the left hand. This is God's proper work (*opus proprium)*, the work of His right hand, which alone renders pointless and superfluous His *opus alienum,* His strange work, His work on the left hand.[173]

In Christ there is a new human subject, there is the true man beside and outside whom God does not know any other, beside and outside whom there is no other.[174]

The rejection of the man on the left hand is done for the sake of the acceptance of the man on the right.

The Eschatological Limit to the Final Judgment: Christological Universalism

1. *Barth's christological Universalism: not an abstract system but a concrete, dynamic reality.*

In his *Epistle to the Romans* we already see Barth's concept of Universalism: a christological Universalism. Here he speaks of the unlimited freedom of God in the light of the decisive death of Christ upon the Cross.[175] We cannot speak of a definite and analyzable number of men. Men who are saved are signs of the light in which all men stand in Christ. They are an eschatological quantity, embracing potentially the totality of psychologically analyzable individuals, whether they belong to the Church or not because the Lord knows His own.[176]

There is an unlimited number known by God. Barth reinterprets the story of Elijah and the 7,000. The 7,000 are not so many individuals. As one whole, they represent the vast, mighty, invisible host, encompassing the lonely Elijah. As only 7,000 as a diminished number, they represent invisibly the whole people of God in their quality as objects of Election in the midst of rejection; they represent the invisible Church of Jacob in the midst of the Church of Esau. The 7,000 are the people of God whom He has not cast off. The answer of God to Elijah does not mean that there are a number of men who know God, but that there is no limit to the number of those who are known by Him. It does not mean that there are just 7,000 men upon whom God has mercy. It means that his mercy is infinite. It does not mean that there exists a calculable number of men who are at peace within themselves. It means that the Oneness of God triumphs over the whole questionableness of the history of the Church.[177] In the *Epistle to the Romans* we see Barth's theistic, christological, supralapsarian approach in the doctrine of Election.

Does this mean that Barth's doctrine of Election is simply another form of Universalism? Barth is not an absolute universalist. His system is not an abstract system, a mechanical one but a concrete, dynamic reality. He sees the Election of each individual as an opening up and enlargement of the closed circle of the Election of Jesus Christ and His community in relation to the world. The existence of each elect means a hidden but real crossing of frontiers, to the gain of the kingdom of God. It is the concern of God that there should be these frontier-crossings. It is also His concern how and when they should take place. It is also His concern what should be the end of these frontier-crossings, which are many in relation to the unworthiness of all men, or few in relation to the great numbers of mankind. It is His concern what is to be the final extent of the circle. Barth adds that if we are to respect the freedom of divine grace, we cannot venture the statement that it must and will finally be coincident with the world of man as such as in the doctrine of the so-called *apokatastasis* (universal reconciliation of all things with God in the consummation). No such right or necessity can legitimately be deduced. As the gracious God does not need to elect or call any single man, so He does not need to elect or call all mankind. His Election and calling do not rise to any historical metaphysics but only to the necessity of attesting them on the ground that they have taken place in Jesus Christ and His community. On the other hand, Barth contends, we cannot venture the opposite statement that there cannot and will not be this final opening up and enlargement of the circle of Election. Neither as the Election of Jesus Christ, the Election of His community, nor the Election of the individual do we know the divine Election of grace as anything other than a decision of His loving-kindness. Otherwise we would be developing an opposing historical metaphysics if we were to try to attribute any limits and therefore an end of these frontier-crossings. Barth avoids both statements in his doctrine of Election because he considers them both abstract and therefore cannot be any part of the message of Christ, but only formal conclusions without any actual substance.[178]

Does not this approach of Barth seem to conflict with his thesis that Jesus Christ is the only man rejected by God? Does this not automatically open up the circle of Election to all men?

Once again Barth answers in christological fashion. He says that we cannot follow the classical doctrine and make the open number of those who are elect in Jesus Christ into a closed number to which all other men are opposed as if they were rejected. First we look to the real and revealed will of God in Jesus Christ. We cannot reckon with another divine rejection than the rejection whose subject was Jesus Christ. Jesus Christ is the irreversible way from the depths to the heights, from death to life. Jesus Christ will not reject any who come to Him. And yet it is not legitimate to make the limitless many of the elect in Jesus Christ the totality of all men. For in Jesus Christ we have to do with the living and personal and therefore the free will of God in relation to the world and every man. We must not and may not take account of any freedom of God which is not that of His real and revealed love in Jesus Christ.[179]

Barth seems to be saying that there is a Universalism but it is a christological Universalism. As long as we look at Jesus Christ as the Electing God, the Elect Man and the very decree of God we are theoretically universalists but we have no right to turn this into an abstract statement for we are dealing with the living God who is continually the predestinating God.

We cannot consider the number of the elect as limited, for we can never find any reason for such a limitation in Jesus Christ.[180]

Barth recognizes that nowhere does the New Testament

say that the world is saved, and we cannot say it without doing violence to the New Testament.[181]

Barth's doctrine of Election is not an abstract universal system which is either closed or open as such. If it is a kind of Universalism then it can only correctly be described as a christological Universalism grounded in the freedom of God who is the Electing God.

2. *Barth's Solution concerning the question of the final Reprobation of the Individual.*

Barth takes a look at the question concerning the final destiny or final loss of the Individual which can be variously described as reprobation, rejection, eternal damnation. He takes an illustration from the New Testament of a man seemingly eternally lost. He studies the case of Judas Iscariot, who betrayed Christ for thirty pieces of silver and then committed suicide.

After having described Jesus as for Judas and Judas as against Jesus, Barth comes to the conclusion that the New Testament gives us no direct information about the outcome of this extraordinary "for and against." It does not describe Judas' repentance in such a way that we may draw an irresistible or even a probable conclusion as to a final and conclusive conversion of Judas in this life. Neither does the New Testament open up for us any prospect of the completion of such a conversion in the hereafter. Nor does it say anything about the inadmissibility of such a conversion. It does not make use of Judas as a plain and specific example of hopeless rejection and perdition, an embodiment of the temporal and eternal rejection of certain men. It emphasizes the unambiguous contrast on both sides. On the one hand, it places no limits to the Grace of Jesus Christ even with regard to Judas. It sets Judas against the brightest radiance of this Grace. On the other hand, it does not use even a single word to suggest that Judas is an example of *apokatastasis*. Barth believes that the situation between Jesus and Judas is only a heightened form of the situation between Jesus and all men—between God's Election of man, and his necessary rejection. The situation is one of open proclamation.[182]

The practical result of all this is that the Church will not then preach an *apokatastasis* or universal reconciliation, nor will it preach a powerless Grace of Jesus Christ or a wickedness of man which is too powerful for it. The Church will preach the overwhelming power of Grace and the weakness of human wickedness in the face of it. This is how the "for" of Jesus and the "against" of Judas undoubtedly confront one another. We do not know whether it led to the conversion of Judas or not, but this is how it always is in the situation of proclamation. Barth comes to the final conclusion that in the New Testament the divine determination of the rejected is unambiguously clear even, and especially in the person of Judas and in his act because the rejected cannot escape this situation and escape its relation of opposites.[183]

Now we come to what seems to me to be the greatest contribution of Karl Barth to the whole question of the damnation of the individual. This is the distinction which Barth makes concerning the rejection or damnation of Jesus Christ and the rejection or damnation of the individual.

Barth defines hell as follows:

> The hell into which the rejected are cast, with all its eternal fire and wailing and gnashing of teeth, consists in the fact that every one finds, and necessarily is and has that which he looked for in his folly and wickedness, that every one has to lie on the bed which he has made himself. This as such is the eternal torment which they must suffer, the eternal death which they have incurred. And at a first glance we may say that Jesus Christ did not suffer this, since it was in obedience that He humbled Himself unto death. But what follows from this obvious incongruity between His action and His suffering? It is certainly not that He suffered something different from the torment and death, the fate, which the rejected have earned and prepared for themselves. It is rather that He suffered this torment and death, this fate, which by His obedience He had not earned or prepared for Himself, for them, in the place of these rejected.[184]

This means that whatever men have suffered who have been delivered and whatever those who have been handed over have deserved to suffer and may still have to suffer, they do not have to suffer that which Jesus Christ suffered. Jesus Christ has suffered for them that which they are spared by His suffering, that which God has therefore spared them by not sparing His own Son.[185]

Barth has given us a christological interpretation of hell. Jesus Christ as the rejected One of God has tasted to the depth all that rejection means and necessarily involves. Barth says that those who are handed over to the wrath of God do not possess an independent reality and status and fate. This reality and status is limited by the status and fate of Jesus Christ. In faith in Jesus Christ we shall never cease to leave wholly and utterly to God the decision about us and all other men. Therefore in faith in Jesus Christ we cannot consider any of those who are handed over by God as lost. It is Barth's contention that we know of none whom God has wholly and exclusively abandoned to himself. We know only of One who was abandoned in this way, only of One who was lost. This One is Jesus Christ. And He was lost and found again that none should be lost apart from Him. The Scriptures, then, according to Barth, tell us what happened to those who were handed over by the wrath of God and abandoned to themselves, to Satan, only as an approximation to the suffering of Christ, fulfilled to their own salvation and at an infinite distance from this suffering. We can understand it only as a kind of terrible warning or reminiscence, as a sign of the death of Christ, and therefore indeed as a sign of damnation which man has deserved, but above all as a sign of the Grace by which he is saved from this damnation.[186]

Barth proceeds now to the concept of the eschatological limitation of the wrath of God in relation to the damnation of individual men on the basis of the rejection or damnation of Jesus Christ. He speaks, however, of eschatological limitation of the wrath and Judgment of God as only an eschatological possibility. This is an important point to consider in all the relevant passages in Scripture on the final Judgment and the wrath of God.[187]

If we look at Scripture, says Barth, then we see that Scripture speaks of countless men, as it does of Judas, in such a way that we must assume that they have lived and died without the possibility, let alone the fulfilment, of any saving repentance. If there is also light for them, and hope, it can only be because and if there is an *eschaton,* a limit, by which even their inescapable bondage is hemmed in from outside.[188]

There is in Barth's doctrine of Election a twofold limitation on the damnation of individual men. The first is the limitation given by the rejection of Jesus Christ. They cannot be rejected as Jesus Christ was rejected. The second limitation is an eschatological one. Whatever men suffer as they are handed over to the wrath of God may have a limit. If this is so then we can see beyond the *eschaton* to a final reconciliation with God, a final restoration of all men and all things to God through the rejection of Jesus Christ. This would be pure christological Universalism. Here there would be a perfect correspondence between the decree of God, the Election of Grace and the final reconciliation of all men to God. But Barth refers to the *eschaton* as only a possibility, but as a christological possibility. Barth wants no system even if it be a logical one. He wants to be loyal to the witness of Scripture and remain with the concrete, dynamic concepts of the Person of Jesus and the living God.

Yet, I would press Barth on his distinction between the damnation of individual men and the damnation of Jesus Christ. If Jesus Christ is the only man rejected by God, if Nothingness has no eternal continuance but is defeated and has no ontological status, and if there is a distinction between the man on the left hand of God who is lost and the man on the right hand of God who is saved, and if there is no eternal dualism, no eternal kingdom opposed to the Kingdom of God, then it seems to me that ultimately Barth must assert the full significance of his christological Universalism. Barth has not watered down the concept of damnation. He has brought out its terrifying significance. He has pointed us to damnation as christologically defined. He has spoken of the possibility of damnation, he has spoken of its eschatological limit. There is a definite distinction between the meaning of hell, damnation and rejection for man and its meaning for Jesus Christ in Barth's doctrine of Election.

Chapter V

A CRITIQUE OF BARTH'S THEOLOGICAL METHODOLOGY

Barth as a Free Theologian

1. *Barth's use of the Bible as a free Theologian.*

In order to properly evaluate Barth's thesis in his doctrine of Election that Jesus Christ is the only Man rejected by God we must look at Barth's theological methodology. Barth describes himself as a free theologian. As a free theologian Barth has a pluralistic approach to theological questions in contrast with other theologians who seemingly have adopted a particular approach in methodology such as Paul Tillich who employs ontological concepts and Rudolf Bultmann who employs existential concepts according to Heidegger's existential analysis. Barth's theological methodology can be described as christological pluralism which includes dialectical thinking. In the final analysis Barth's theology is a theology of the Word of God. This is the way he has described his theology.

Karl Barth, however, does not start with a doctrine of the canon and verbal inspiration of Holy Scripture. But neither does Barth start with the so-called "ascertained results" of historical-critical research, or the so-called "exegetical findings." He points out that these results have a tendency to change every thirty years and from one exegete to another. Barth further contends that analysis of both Biblical and secular texts does not guarantee that we are really listening. Barth uses the method of combining in one single act analysis and synthesis in his reading and studies.[189]

Barth speaks of Christian doctrine as legitimately grounded and rightly developed and expounded when it is understood and explained as a part of the responsibility laid upon the hearing and teaching Church towards the self-revelation of God attested in Holy Scripture. The doctrine of Election then is a form of an exposition of what God Himself has said and still says.

Barth then speaks of the witness of Scripture to the revelation of God. This then is for Barth the authority of Scripture. Barth rejects that use of the Bible which simply gives a supplementary proof side by side with reason. In this way one can arrive at the view that the doctrine of the Bible is identical with Calvinism, or Lutheranism.[190]

According to Barth we must not come to the Bible with a question dictated to us by experience, i.e., with a presupposition which has only an empirical basis, in order then to understand the statements of the Bible as an answer to this question, which means chiefly as a confirmation of the presupposition which underlies the question. In this way we could be led to judge men's external relationship to the Gospel and arrive at the doctrine of double Predestination.[191]

Those who have a strict fundamentalist viewpoint and who accept Verbal inspiration will immediately dismiss Barth's view of Scripture as a witness to the revelation of God. The Lutheran Church-Missouri Synod as a confessional Church body accepts the doctrine of Verbal Inspiration and identifies the Bible with the Revelation of God. Barth teaches that Jesus Christ is the Word of God and the Bible becomes the Word of God in so far as it has to do with Jesus Christ who is the Revelation of God.

Barth's methodology involves his concept of christological thinking.

2. *Barth's christological Thinking.*

Barth's theological methodology is not that of a principle or system of theological thought such as "The Triumph of Grace." Barth feels that we cannot control God or Jesus Christ with principles and abstract systems of thought. Over against all principles and systems of thought Barth presents the living, acting, concrete Person of Jesus Christ. This is what he means by christological thinking. We cannot control the function of Jesus Christ. As a free Theologian Barth begins with Jesus Christ. This means the recognition of the resurrection of Jesus Christ as the direction for his reasoning.[192]

Barth argues strongly for christological thinking and has a running dialogue with Berkouwer over this matter. Barth's formal definition of christological thinking is as follows:

> I can only speak for myself, and I maintain that for me thinking is christological only when it consists in the perception, comprehension, understanding and estimation of the reality of the living person of Jesus Christ as attested by Holy Scripture, in attentiveness to the range and significance of His existence, in openness to His self-disclosure, in consistency in following Him as is demanded. In this formal definition I am confident that Berkouwer and I are in agreement and I also think we can agree that christological thinking in this sense is a very different process from deduction from a given principle. I underline, however, that we are not dealing with a Christ-principle, but with Jesus Christ Himself as attested by Holy Scripture.[193]

In this respect Barth has an ally in Brunner who declares that a falsely objective interpretation of the New Testament words about judgment led to the belief in a double decree. If we are to understand the Judgment, we must start with the centre of faith, from the unconditional love of God known in Jesus Christ. The double decree interpretation made Judgment itself the starting-point and consequently the bestowal of Grace in Christ was degraded to the status of a cause of the double conclusion of history. At the decisive point christocentric thinking was abandoned and was replaced partly by a false exegesis of the Bible, partly by natural theology.[194]

Berkouwer had spoken of Barth's system of Theology as the "Triumph of Grace." Barth objects to this because it might give rise to the impression that what is meant is the victory of one principle, that of Grace, over another which is to be described as evil, sin, the devil or death. Barth is not concerned with the precedence, victory or triumph of a principle, even though the principle be that of Grace. Barth is concerned with the living person of Jesus Christ. Strictly speaking, it is not Grace, but He Himself as its Bearer, Bringer and Revealer who is the Victory. Barth prefers to speak of "Jesus is Victor" as the theme of his system rather than "The Triumph of Grace." [195]

Barth's christological thinking seems to be a form of dialectical thinking. To a philosopher dialectical thinking is a method of reasoning, that is, the doctrine of opposites.[196] This we see in Plato, Hegel, etc. Jocz says that for the theologian dialectic is not a method which yields results, or a system of reasoning in which life can be resolved in concepts, but a situation in which man is challenged to act and does act in faith or disobedience.[197]

Barth is a dialectical theologian. He employs a method of reasoning and at the same time he wishes to respond in faith and in obedience to the revelation of God in Holy Scripture, so that his theology is not a theological system of logical abstract thought. The living concrete Person of Jesus Christ reveals Himself as the One Who is both the Electing God and the Elect Man. Barth's understanding of the Word of God, his response to what he hears God say in His Word leads him to formulate a doctrine of opposites in Election which have a christological unity such as that Jesus Christ is both the Elect Man and the only Man rejected by God.

As a free theologian Barth does not deny his indebtedness to a particular philosophy or ontology, to ways of thought and speech. Barth maintains that no one speaks exclusively in Biblical terms. His ontology will be subject to criticism and control by his theology, and not conversely. He will not necessarily feel obligated to the philosophical *kairos,* the latest prevailing philosophy.[198]

Barth's use of christological thinking includes then the philosophic method of dialectical thinking. Instead of a concept we have challenge in man's encounter with the living God. This results in Barth's use of the term possibility. The condemnation of man is only a possibility, only a threat. Man stands under the threat and danger of being damned. His condemnation hangs over him like a sword. But his condemnation is not yet pronounced. There is still only the threat and menace of it. But these are real enough. God has not yet condemned man. God could do this today or tomorrow. The threat has not yet been fulfilled. The sword has not yet fallen. The danger is still only a danger. Man is not yet damned. He is not yet lost.[199]

If man is not damned then it can only be a matter of the unexpected work of Grace. Furthermore, Barth says that we cannot expect or maintain an *apokatastasis* or universal reconciliation as the goal and end of all things. No such postulate can be made even though we appeal to the cross and resurrection of Jesus Christ, even though theological consistency might seem to lead Barth's and our thoughts most clearly in this direction. We must not arrogate to ourselves that which can be given and received only as a free gift.[200]

Yet, there is the possibility that in the reality of God and man in Jesus Christ there is contained much more than we might expect and therefore the supremely unexpected withdrawal of that final threat, that is, that in the truth of this reality there might be contained the super-abundant promise of the final deliverance of all men. There is no good reason why we should not be open to this possibility.[201]

Dialectical thinking leads Barth to indirect revelation instead of direct revelation. Van Til criticizes Barth on this score that if God had bound himself to a direct revelation in history, given to some men only, then He could speak no word of Yes to all men everywhere. If revelation were to be identified with any fact of history, then this revelation would be the possession of some men and not of all. The indirectness of the communication of God's Grace involves for Barth, the universality, because of the originality of the Yes of God toward all men.[202]

Van Til accuses Barth of cancelling out at every point of God's revelation its clarity and dependability. On Barth's view, there is no meaning to either the threats or the promises of God. He further states that Barth wants no God who reveals Himself clearly and directly through Christ in history and that his exegesis of Scripture is controlled by the *a priori* condition that the Bible cannot reveal such a God.[203]

Van Til overlooks the fact that with Barth history starts in eternity, before the Creation of the world, in the eternal decree of God. Secondly, Barth looks at the concrete person of Jesus Christ, to the particular event of God's self-revelation in Jesus Christ. Barth never theologizes *in abstracto* but *in concreto*.[204]

As Hartwell points out, with Barth it is always a question first of reality, on the basis of faith, and of text (the relevant passages of the Bible) and then a question of exegesis and interpretation.[205]

Barth's methodology has certain advantages over past systems in the area of christological and dialectical thinking:

a. Barth's system has an advantage which we can describe as a Dogmatic advantage. His doctrine of Election and his system of theology as a whole is more flexible. He is not tied down to one particular answer. There are given possibilities, hopes and expectations with regard to the salvation of all mankind missing in previous systems of Election.

b. This methodology frees him from being contradicted by a particular passage in Scripture. All the other systems such as Calvinism, Lutheranism and Universalism can find Scriptural support and an exegetical basis but they do not find complete support because one can always find passages to contradict a particular system or doctrine of Election.

c. Although Barth cannot give us the absolute assurance of salvation on the basis of his christological Universalism and therefore does not seem to have advanced beyond Calvin and Luther, he can free himself from the uncertainty in the message preached by Calvin and Luther because he directs us to look only to Jesus Christ, the Electing God, the Elect Man, the Very Decree of Salvation, the only rejected Man. Barth's methodology helps us to avoid the abstract universal systems by a clear distinction between the meaning of rejection for Jesus Christ and for the individual.

d. As a free Theologian Barth can remain within the Church. He speaks and thinks within the Church where there are confessions. He can pay loving respect to these Confessions as guidance in reading, explaining and applying the Scriptures. At the same time he is not bound by them. He will listen to them carefully. He will be free to express what they already have expressed, to express it better if he has the talent to do so. He is equally free to acknowledge their much better formulation of what he wants to say. In the Church a free theologian can be the son and disciple of the fathers such as Luther and Calvin. Yet, he does not have to insist on complete agreement with them. He can respect the freedom of the fathers and let them express their wisdom and then learn from them what in his own freedom he may and can learn from them.[206] Finally, a free theologian works in communication with other theologians.[207]

This gives to Barth's theological methodology the freedom to learn from others and to share with other theologians what one has encountered in the witness of Scripture to the Revelation of God in Christ. This frees Barth from dogmatic arrogance and from the narrow point of view that believes that theology has done its work and there is nothing left for theology to say and do.

There are other alternatives to Barth's theological methodology which consists of christological thinking and dialectical thinking. There is the alternative of a fundamentalistic approach to the Bible and a narrow view of Verbal Inspiration. There is also the alternative of a principle or system of theology in place of the dynamic act of God in Christ.

Question of an Exegetical Basis: A Critique of Barth's Exegetical Approach

1. *Barth's treatment of passages on Election and Judgment.*

Every system on Election claims to have an exegetical or Biblical basis (Augustine, Aquinas, Calvin, Luther, Reformed and Lutheran Orthodoxy of the seventeenth century. Arminianism, Federal Theology, Universalism). This means that every theological system on Election can find an exegetical basis by which to defend its own position as scriptural and regard other systems or positions on the doctrine of Election as unscriptural. At any rate it is necessary to have an exegetical basis for the doctrine of Election. A theologian, even a free theologian, is still under the obligation to bring his doctrinal view or theological position into harmony with the Scriptural witness to the meaning of Election. Barth recognizes this obligation and proceeds to do this.

Barth has given us a critique of the use of the Bible by previous theologians. He states that the older theologians did read their Bibles carefully and that they did intend to comment on Romans 9 to 11 and other passages in the Scriptural witness even as Barth intended to do. The Bible, however, according to Barth, did not impel or constrain them to take the step he was now taking, but confirmed them rather in their positing of a twofold obscurity in respect of God and man at the beginning of all things. They did not find in their reading of the Bible the Electing God and Elected Man.[208]

Barth looks to John 1:1-2 as the basis of his belief that in the beginning, in eternity Jesus was already the Elect Man, the decree of God. This passage obviously speaks of the pre-existence of the Son of God or the Logos and the Deity of the Logos. Barth prefers to speak of Jesus as pre-existent and as God. Barth says: "It is He, Jesus, who is in the beginning with God. It is He who by nature is God. This is what is guaranteed in Jn. 1:1." John does not honor Jesus with the title "Logos" but rather he honours the title by applying it a few lines later as a predicate of Jesus.[209]

In this passage Barth sees Jesus Christ as the eternal will of God, the eternal decree of God and the eternal beginning of God.[210]

This passage also speaks of the Man Jesus. In so doing it asserts that Jesus Christ is Elected Man. In fact all the Johannnine passages which speak of His mission, of His doing the will and work of His Father, of His submission, and of the submission of His people to the rule of the Father, really point to this aspect of the matter.[211]

Is Barth reading more into John 1:1-2 than is really there? Does the passage really speak of the Elect Man and the decree of God? Does it not mainly speak of the pre-existence of the Word and the Deity of the Word? It is possible to do what Barth did with this passage only in connection with other texts. Isolate John 1:1-2 from other election passages and it seems to me that it would be extremely difficult to derive from John 1:1-2 the concepts of Jesus as the decree of God and as the Elected Man.

Barth equates Jesus' electing disciples with Jesus as the Electing God. He says that the passages in John 13:18 and 15:16,19, in which Jesus points to Himself as the One who elects His disciples, are not to be understood loosely but in their strictest and most proper sense. There is no rivalry between the Father and the Son in the Johannine Gospel which can and should be dissolved by subordination. The statement: "All mine are thine," is balanced by the further statement: "Thine are mine" (Jn. 17:10). Jesus was "sent" but He also "came." As He is in the Father, the Father is also in Him (Jn. 14:10). Barth maintains that in the light of these passages the electing of the disciples ascribed to Jesus must be understood not merely as a function undertaken by Him in an instrumental and representative capacity, but rather as an act of divine sovereignty, in which there is seen in a particular way the primal and basic decision of God which is also that of Jesus Christ.[212]

Here Barth has strong Biblical support for his concept of Jesus Christ as the Electing God.

Regarding passages on Election itself, Barth points out that proportionately the passages in the Bible which speak expressly and directly of the divine Election are not very numerous.[213]

A key passage in Barth's doctrine of Election is Ephesians 1:4. Barth sees the main emphasis in the phrase "in Him." God has chosen us in Him. This was before the foundation of the world according to the good-pleasure of his will for the purpose that we might be predestinated unto the adoption of children by Jesus Christ himself. We are elected in Jesus Christ and by or through Him. From this Barth concludes that when we have to do with the reality indicated by the concept of Election or Predestination we are not outside the sphere of the name of Jesus Christ but within it and within the sphere of the unity of very God and very man indicated by this name.[214]

Here is Barth's main proof that Election must not be separated from Christology (Ephesians 1:4).

Barth recognizes that there is no Biblical basis for teaching that the Bible teaches Universalism. The Bible does not deal in totalities or in quantities. In his commentary on Romans 11 in the *Church Dogmatics* Barth clearly affirms that the expression "the fulness of the Gentiles" does not mean the sum total of all Gentile individuals. The Bible nowhere reckons with unqualified totalities of this kind. The sum total of elected members in the body of Christ from the Gentiles' world is the fulness of the Gentiles.[215]

By the same token, "All Israel," does not mean the totality of all Jewish individuals. Barth does not consider

"All Israel" to be a simple parallel to the "fulness of the Gentiles," denoting the totality of the elect numbers of Jesus Christ from the Jews. "All Israel" is the community of those elected by God in and with Jesus Christ both from Jews and also from Gentiles, the whole Church which together with the holy root of Israel will consist in the totality of all the branches finally united with and drawing sustenance from it, in the totality constituted by the remnant continuing in and with the original stem of Jesus Christ, by the wild sheets added later from the Gentiles, and by the branches which were cut off and finally grafted in again.[216]

Barth cannot simply be accused of Universalism; even his christological understanding of Universalism does not permit him to speak in totalities.

Brunner attacks Barth's understanding of Election. He affirms against Barth that in the witness to revelation in the New Testament the Subject of Election is God alone.[217] Brunner agrees that the Son is Election and that apart from the Son there is no Election but he rejects the absolute equation of God and Christ.[218] Election is not something in eternity but rather which in Jesus Christ becomes "Event" in Time.[219]

Brunner regards it a mere theory in Barth's doctrine of Election to speak of the pre-existent Divine-Humanity.

Brunner breaks with Barth on the relationship between Jesus Christ and the Holy Trinity. He believes that there are works of God which as such are precisely not works of the Son. Brunner regards God alone as the Creator and the Son is called simply and solely the Mediator of the Creation. In the New Testament the Son, or Jesus Christ, is never called the Creator. This title is given to the Father alone.[220]

By making the Son the Mediator of Creation and Election rather than the Creator Himself and the Electing God as does Barth, Brunner has introduced the sharpest type of subordinationism into the doctrine of the Trinity and he has introduced the danger of the heresy of Tritheism. Whether Jesus Christ or the Son of God is called Creator directly or not is beside the point. The act of being the Creator or the function of being the Creator is attributed to Jesus Christ in John 1:3. The passage refers to the Pre-

Incarnate Word but the Word became Incarnate according to John 1:14. John 1:13 and John 1:14 refer to the same Person, the Person of the Word. Jesus Christ is one Person in the unity of Godhood and manhood. Whether we are speaking of Jesus Christ as the Incarnate Word of God or whether we are speaking of the Pre-Incarnate Word we are speaking of the same Person. Jesus Christ revealed His consciousness of being in unity with God even before the Creation of the world according to John 17:1-5.

Barth has the Johannine Gospel to support him in his assertion that Jesus Christ is equal to God, is God Himself and that we can therefore speak of Jesus Christ in eternity before Creation. Brunner has also misunderstood Barth's meaning of the pre-existence of the God-Man Jesus Christ because he has not understood the eternal decree of God and its identification with Jesus Christ in the doctrine of Election in Barth's *Church Dogmatics*.

Barth has Biblical support for his views on judgment and christological Universalism. He takes into view that there are passages in the New Testament which speak of hell and everlasting condemnation such as Matthew 5:26; Matthew 25:41, Revelation 19:9, 20:15, 21:8, 22:15. Barth speaks of a final possibility, of an entirely new possibility beyond the completed judgment. There is still the prospect of it, even if in endless remoteness and depth. In support of this eschatological limit Barth refers to I Corinthians 5 which speaks of the delivery of Christians to Satan. Paul says that the flesh must be destroyed. The judgment on his human existence must take its course, as must the final outcome of the fact that he was lost but he does not say this without adding: "so that the spirit may be saved in the day of the Lord." Barth points out a distinction between soul and spirit in Pauline anthropology. The spirit is the invisible spiritual principle of life in human existence. This is the fellowship with Jesus Christ which is given to the Christian at baptism and on the basis of which he has become a new and therefore for the first time a real subject. The flesh as the totality of body and soul of those delivered up is forfeited to the result of the delivery. But Paul did not say that the spirit of this man is forfeited by this handing-over. On the contrary, he said that just because of the handing-over it partakes in future salvation. Paul carried out the handing-over of this man with the express purpose that while his flesh should be destroyed his spirit should be saved.[221]

This lends support to Barth's conception of the man on the left and the right hand of God, of God's strange and proper work. Here we have an example of Barth's theological methodology which I call christological pluralism. The man on the left hand is the man God has rejected. The man on the right hand of God is the man God has accepted. The rejection of the man on the left hand of God is done for the sake of the acceptance of the man on the right hand of God. To speak Biblically we could cite the example of Saul of Tarsus as the man on the left hand of God, the man God has rejected. The Apostle Paul who is Saul of Tarsus converted to Jesus Christ is the man on the right hand of God, the man God has accepted. In like manner the flesh of man as the totality of body and soul is handed over and destroyed for the sake of salvation of the spirit of man which is the new subject as christologically determined.

Barth gives a christological basis for the distinction between the man on the left hand of God and the man on the right hand, between God's strange work and His proper work, between the flesh and spirit of man. These distinctions are christologically unified in the fact that Jesus Christ is both the rejected man and the Elect Man. The act of rejecting, destroying, handing over is done for the sake of electing and saving man. The Yes of God is God's final Word. The No of God is subject to the Yes of God. God's proper work triumphs over His strange work. In Jesus Christ the flesh of man is destroyed that his spirit may be saved.

2. *Main objections to Barth's exegetical approach.*

It is surprising that the sharpest criticism against Barth has come from the theologians of the Reformed faith. Van Til objects to Barth's interpretation of Ephesians 1:4 because Barth limits this passage to teaching that God can only have one attitude toward man and that God cannot righteously punish any man for sin eternally. He objects to Barth's including reprobation as reprobation in Christ. Van Til insists that Scripture teaches that many are called but few are chosen and that he who does not believe is judged already. According to Scripture (Jesus, the epistles of the apostles, the Revelation of John) reprobation means to be outside of Christ, and this totally, subjectively and objectively. Scripture does not teach that reprobation stands under the control of Election. In conformity with Calvinism Van Til emphasizes over against Barth that Christ shed his blood for His people.[222]

Clark is also dissatisfied with Barth's so-called ambiguous use of Bible passages on Damnation. He says that Barth shows both little caution and even a little irritation at the mention of Universalism. There is, nevertheless, a strong tendency in Barth toward universal salvation despite the fact that one can discover definite statements in Barth that some people are eternally lost and will never enter heaven, but suffer always in hell. The doubtful passages might clumsily be fitted in somehow.[223]

Van Til and Clark overlook Barth's distinction between the damnation of individual men and the damnation of Jesus Christ and the distinction between the man on the left hand of God and the man on the right hand of God. God's attitude toward sin and the sinner is not limited to only one viewpoint. God does reject sin and the man on the left hand. Barth does not deny that there are passages on judgment and damnation. Barth, however, does not limit himself to a select number of Bible passages. A study of his *Church Dogmatics* reveals the tremendous exegetical study Barth has made on the question of Election and Damnation. He also brings to his exegetical studies christological thinking. He sees Election and Damnation in the light of Christology.

3. *Barth's attitude to Scripture.*

Van Til points out that Reformed theologians object to Barth's denial that Scripture is the direct revelation of God and therefore the Christ of Barth is not the Christ of Scripture. Clark supports Van Til on this point and says that Orthodox Protestantism equates the Bible with the Word of God and that this does not hold to Barth's thinking.[224]

Barth does not deny that Scripture is the Word of God in his theological system. Barth speaks of Jesus Christ, the Scriptures and the preached Word as the Word of God. What Barth objects to is a particular view of the inspiration of Scripture. Barth holds to a dynamic concept of the Bible as the Word of God.

4. *Ambiguous use of Scripture in other Election systems.*

Why should Barth be faulted as not taking seriously passages on damnation? Augustine and Calvin have also variously interpreted the same passage in order that it might be able to fit in with their scheme of double Predestination. In commenting on I Timothy 2:4 Augustine says that the expression "He wills all men to be saved" may be understood in many ways in order to harmonize with his view that not all men are saved. It may mean the following:

a. All the predestined will be saved.
b. Every kind of man is found among the predestined.
c. We ourselves wish all men to be saved.[225]

Calvin interprets I Timothy 2:4 as meaning that "all" refers not to individuals but to orders of men in their various civil and national vocations.[226]

Boettner says that the word "will" as used in I Timothy 2:4 is used in different senses in Scripture. It can mean decree, purpose, desire, wish. On this basis we could translate I Timothy 2:4 to mean that God wishes or desires the salvation of all men or that He decrees and purposes their salvation.[227]

By the same token the word "all" is used in different sense in Scripture. In some cases it does mean every individual.[228] In some instances the word "all" is used in order to teach that the Gospel is for the Gentiles as well as for the Jews.[229]

Another example of different meanings of a word which can change the sense of a passage is the word "world." In John 2:2 it is said that Christ died not for our sins only but for the sins of the whole world. In John 12:47 Christ came to save the world. The world means the race. When John the Baptist said, "Behold the Lamb of God that taketh away the sin of the world!" this did not contradict the doctrine of "Limited Atonement," since John was preaching to sinners and not to saints who alone could have understood that Christ died only for the elect and not for the non-elect.[230]

Sometimes the term "world" means only a part of the world as when it says that the Devil is the deceiver of the whole world or that the whole world lies in the evil one (John 5:19). World can sometimes mean the believing world or the Christian Church.[231]

Boettner interprets John 3:16 as meaning that redemption is universal as to space, that God loved the world as a whole and that this is the true Universalism of the Scriptures: the universal Christianization of the world and the complete defeat of the forces of spiritual wickedness. This does not mean that every individual will be saved, for many are lost.[232]

All this shows that people can find Universalism or Limited Atonement or eternal rejection in the scriptures and can quote one set of passages against each other. One system can quote passages in favor of Universalism, another can find passages to support Judgment and rejection.

Barth's exegetical approach has the following advantages:

1. Barth does not set passages on Judgment against Universalism or Universalism against Judgment. He is not interested in logical consistency primarily but obedience to what he hears in the witness of Scripture to the revelation of God in Jesus Christ.

2. He finds a great number of possibilities in Scripture such as the meaning of rejection as applied to Jesus Christ and to the individual. Although there is an exegetical basis for all these possibilities they are all under the control of christological thinking.

3. All of this frees Barth from being bound to one particular answer in the doctrine of Election. There is christological pluralism in Barth's doctrine of Election: The freedom of God, new decisions, eschatological limit, the rejection of Jesus Christ and the rejection of the individual man, rejection of an eternal dualism, rejection of the power of evil or sin to limit the grace of God, distinction between the flesh of man and the spirit of man, distinction between the man on the left hand of God and the man on the right hand of God, the case of Judas Iscariot is ambiguous, Jesus is Victor.

Barth has gone into great exegetical detail throughout his *Church Dogmatics*. He has done his home work. It would be beyond the purpose of this thesis to make a comparative analysis of Barth's exegesis in the doctrine of Election or Judgment and compare it with other theological systems.

I should like to close this chapter with a reference to several passages in the Old and New Testament which seem to me to substantiate Barth's exegetical approach. God threatens condemnation to man but as Barth says it has not yet happened, it can still be removed. In Exodus 32 the Lord tells Moses that He is about to consume the nation Israel because they are a stiffnecked people. Moses pleads with the Lord on behalf of the people. We are told that Yahweh repented of the evil which He thought to do unto His people.

In the fifteenth chapter of St. Paul's second epistle to the Corinthians we find a prophecy of the final consummation of all things: The Resurrection of the dead, the manifestation of Christ as triumphant over all His enemies, death itself is destroyed. At that time Christ as the Son delivers up the Kingdom to God the Father and then is Himself subject to Him Who put all things under Him that God may be all in all. Is this not a proclamation of christological Universalism in the New Testament? Is this not a vision of the manifestation at the end of time of God's victory over every evil: sin, death and hell? Does this not tell us that the beginning and end of all the ways and works of God are the ways and works of Grace? Is not Jesus finally victor? How then can there be an eternal dualism, an ontological realm of godlessness opposed to God?

In Philippians 2 Paul says that every knee in the universe shall bow and every tongue shall confess that Jesus Christ is Lord to the glory of God the Father. Does this not suggest an eschatological limit to the wrath of God and the suffering of hell and exclude an eternal dualism?

In Barth's exegetical approach one finds room for the wrath of God, for rejection and damnation and for the final victory of Jesus over sin, death and hell.

Chapter VI

A CRITIQUE OF THE CHRISTOLOGICAL CONTENT OF BARTH'S DOCTRINE OF ELECTION: THEOLOGICAL HARMONIZATION

1. *The Incarnation and Jesus as the Only Rejected Man of God.*

What is the relationship between the Incarnation and Jesus Christ as the only Man rejected by God in Barth's doctrine of Election? Barth speaks of the whole Incarnate state on earth as the obedience of the Son of God, as the way of the Son of God into the far country, as the time when the Lord became a Servant. The eternal Son of the eternal Father became obedient by offering and humbling Himself to be the brother of man, to take His place with the transgressor, to judge him by judging Himself and dying in His place. God the Father raised His Son from the dead and in so doing recognized and gave effect to His death and passion as a satisfaction made for us, as our conversion to God, and therefore as our redemption from death to life.[233]

Barth gives us a penetrating analysis of what it meant for Jesus Christ to be incarnate. The coming of Jesus Christ into the flesh is the bearing of our rejection. The term flesh in the language of both the New and Old Testaments means man standing under the divine verdict and judgment, whose existence has already become nothing, man who is a sinner and must perish before God. "Flesh" is the concrete form of human nature and the being of man in his world under the sign of the fall of Adam—the being of man as corrupted, destroyed, unreconciled with God and therefore lost. On the basis of II Corinthians 5:21 where it is said that God made Christ to be sin for us, He who knew no sin,

Barth points out how throughout the New Testament Jesus is regarded and treated as a sinner. People thought Jesus was insane (Mk. 3:21), demon-possessed (Mk. 3:22), a gluttonous man and a winebibber, a friend of publicans and sinners (Mt. 11:19), a deceiver of the people (Jn. 7:12), a blasphemer of God (Mt. 9:3; 26:65), there is suspicion concerning His birth (Mt. 1:19). At His baptism He appears as a penitent in solidarity with other penitents (Mt. 3:15), He is crucified between two thieves (Mt. 27:28). Barth concludes by saying that according to the New Testament the Heidelberg Catechism is quite right when in Question 37 it says that during the whole time of His life on earth Jesus bore the wrath of God against the sin of the whole human race.[234]

According to Barth the Incarnation is to be seen as Jesus' existence in the flesh under the wrath of God. In double Predestination Barth has said that God elects Himself to rejection and damnation and elects man to salvation. This is the meaning of Incarnation. Good Scriptural support for this is found in the great christological hymn of St. Paul in Philippians chapter 2 when Paul speaks of the *kenosis* of Christ, the great self-emptying. His self-emptying could not be the loss of Godhead but rather is the freedom of God to go into the far country, to be under the wrath of God and the curse of the Law.

This is the concrete Deity of Christ. Barth says that God as God is able and willing and ready to condemn and humble Himself in this way and that this is the mystery of the Deity of Christ.[235]

In the Incarnation we have to do with this new mystery of God being against Himself. There is a cleft or rift or gulf in God Himself, between His being and essence in Himself and His activity and work as the Reconciler of the world. God does not alter Himself, but He denies the immutability of His being, to be in discontinuity with Himself, to be against Himself. The Incarnation means that God is against God in His free will. He exercised His mercy that way.[236] In Philippians 2 Paul says that Christ did not consider His equality with God something to be displayed as a prize or booty but rather He emptied Himself.

Barth quotes Mark 15:34 as the meaning of the Incarnation: "My God, My God, why hast thou forsaken me?"[237] The purpose of the Incarnation was not only that God should become man but that He should overcome flesh by becoming flesh Himself and reconcile the world unto Himself as He is in Christ.[238]

There is theological harmonization between the New Testament view of the Incarnation, its meaning and purpose, and Barth's concept of Jesus Christ as the only Man rejected by God. We must remember, however, that in Barth's doctrine of Election Jesus Christ as the only Man rejected by God has various meanings and possibilities as we have seen.

2. *The Vicarious Atonement and Jesus as the Only Man rejected by God.*

The Vicarious Atonement means that Jesus in substitutionary fashion does for us and in our place what we could not do for ourselves. He made atonement for our sins and satisfied the wrath and righteousness of the Holy God. One can quote many passages from the Scriptures such as Isaiah 53 and Romans 3 to prove that one aspect of Jesus' work was the Vicarious Atonement. Anselm was a mighty proponent of this view in the Church. The Vicarious Atonement is one of the traditions in the Church in its understanding of the meaning of Jesus' death on the Cross at Golgotha.

Barth emphatically affirms that Jesus Christ took the place of man and in his place rendered that obedience which is required of the covenant partner of God. He did it by taking to Himself the sins of all men. He freely offered Himself as the sacrifice which had to be made when God vindicated Himself in relation to man by choosing to suffer the wrath of God in His own body and the fire of His love in His own soul. He took the place of all men.[239] If Jesus Christ really took the place of all men then Jesus Christ is really the only rejected Man of God. Then there is no such thing as a limited atonement. Men may suffer the wrath of God but they cannot suffer what Jesus suffered.

Jesus underwent the Judgment under which we had passed. In this way He was for us. All the judgment and accusation that fell upon us happened in the Person of His

Son. Jesus is the Judge who was Judged. This is the way Barth understands the Vicarious Atonement. This fits in with his concept of the double decree. God elects Himself to damnation which is the same as the Judge is Judged. Barth, too, asks the question: *"Cur Deus Homo?"* It is in order that God as man might do and accomplish and achieve and complete all this for us wrong-doers, in order that in this way there might be brought about by Him our reconciliation with Him and conversion to Him.[240]

Barth ties this in with the Electing God and Elect Man. He who is in the one person the Electing God and the one Elect Man is as the rejecting God, the God who judges sin in the flesh in His own person the one rejected Man.[241] This is in harmony with the words of St. Paul: "To wit, that God was in Christ, reconciling the WORLD unto Himself, not imputing their trespasses unto them; and hath committed unto us the word of reconciliation . . . For He hath made Him to be sin for us, who knew no sin; that we might be made the righteousness of God in Him." (2 Cor. 5:19-21).

Barth further argues that if Jesus Christ came and took our place as the Representative of our evil case, then there is nothing more that we can seek and do there as evildoers.[242]

The Vicarious Atonement according to Barth is an ontological atonement. In His own Person Jesus Christ has made an end of us as sinners and therefore of sin itself by going to death as the One who took our place. In His person He has delivered up us sinners and sin itself to destruction. He has removed us sinners and sin, negated us, cancelled us out: ourselves, our sin, and the accusation, condemnation and perdition which had overtaken us. The man of sin, the first Adam, the cosmos alienated from God, the present evil world, was taken and killed and buried in and with Him on the cross. Jesus Christ is the one great sinner in this sense.[243]

How then can there be anyone not included in the reconciliation with God? The man on the left hand of God is cancelled out. There is now only the man on the right hand of God. The Vicarious Atonement is an ontological reconciliation. There is nothing beyond the reach of Christ's atoning death.

Barth quotes Luke 15:3ff to show that Jesus is the one lost sheep, the one lost coin, the lost son and therefore as the Judge He is the One who is judged.[244]

3. *The Final Judgment and Jesus Christ as the only Man rejected by God.*

One can find theological harmonization between the Incarnation and Jesus Christ as the only Man rejected by God, between the Vicarious Atonement and Jesus Christ as the only Man rejected by God in Barth's doctrine of Election. Can one find theological harmonization between the final judgment and Jesus Christ as the only Man rejected by God?

Barth proposes that there is unity in the work of God. There cannot be another divine intervention, which is foreign to the divine action in Jesus Christ. No work of God is independent of His work as Lord of the covenant and as the Reconciler of the world. Even the new act of God in which He introduced the genuine beyond of the judgment, end and death which comes on man in Jesus Christ must, like this event, be an event which takes place by and in and to Jesus Christ.[245]

How does Barth reconcile Christ's coming as the Judge of all men at the end of time with Jesus Christ as the only Man rejected by God? Barth knows that when the Son of God comes and sets some on His right hand and others on His left hand, He comes to call the world and therefore all men and every individual man to render an account and to make an answer for its condition. But he points out that all men will be measured by the One who is man as they are under the same presuppositions and conditions. In His light they will be shown for what they are and what they are not. With His existence there will fall upon them in all its concreteness the decision, the divine and ultimate decision.[246]

We must remember that Barth speaks of the distinction between the damnation of Jesus Christ and the damnation of individual men, of the eschatological limitation of the wrath of God. This can be made to harmonize with the picture of Jesus Christ as Judge as well as the view that it is the man on the left hand who is being rejected.

Luther spoke of the Atonement in terms not only of sacrifice but also in terms of victory over the tyrants: sin, death, hell, Law, the wrath of God. Is this not the meaning of Jesus the Judge at the end of the world?

From an objective point of view Barth's thesis that Jesus Christ is the only Man rejected by God can harmonize with the New Testament witness to the meaning of the Incarnation, the Vicarious Atonement and the Final Judgment.

Chapter VII

QUESTION OF INTERNAL CONSISTENCY IN BARTH'S DOCTRINE OF ELECTION (DOGMATIC CONTINUITY)

1. *Problem of the relationship between Election and Universalism.*

There appears to be a contradiction in Barth's doctrine of Election between his view of Jesus Christ as the only Man rejected by God and his refusal to speak of the salvation of every individual man, of absolute Universalism. On the one hand there is in Barth's doctrine of Election such elements as the decree, no dualism in God, ontological reconciliation, the man on the left hand and on the right hand of God, the distinction between the rejection of Jesus Christ and the rejection of individual men, the flesh of man and the spirit of man. On the other hand there is the freedom of God, new decisions, possibility of damnation. There then appears to be a logical inconsistency in Barth to affirm the totality of salvation for all men.

We must, however, remember that in speaking of the damnation of individual men and the damnation of Jesus Christ Barth says that there is an eschatological limit to the damnation of men and that men cannot suffer the rejection which Jesus Christ suffered. This is the great contribution of Barth to the meaning of damnation in the Bible. This means that Barth is free from denying the possibility of damnation as taught by Matthew chapter 25, and is free from the abstract system of Universalism which teaches universal salvation without a christological foundation. Barth's thesis that Jesus Christ is the only Man rejected by God leads to an ultimate christological Universalism.

Weber concludes that even in Barth's system there is a final question, an ultimate mystery.[247] Hartwell points out that Barth believes in a higher divine grace or logic which surpasses the logic of finite human mind which leaves the question of the salvation of all men an open one.[248] Matczak believes that apokatastasis or Universalism logically follows from Barth's position.[249] Van Til takes note of the difference between Barth's "Biblical Universalism" and Philosophical Universalism. Biblical Universalism according to Barth is not based upon man's inherent goodness and unlike the philosophical Universalism of Leibniz wants to take sin seriously.[250] According to Van Til Barth is caught between a principle of continuity based on the idea of timeless being and a principle of discontinuity based on the idea of pure contingency.[251] There is in Barth a realm of chance and a tendency toward Universalism according to Van Til. Berkouwer says that Barth's clear rejection of the *apokatastasis* sets up a tension between the omnipotence of the divine decision and the problem of faith and unbelief on the other hand.[252] Barth stands at a crossroads in his thinking. He can move to the right or to the left, not in terms of the demands of a logical system, but in terms of centrally religious considerations. The one way that is open is that of the *apokatastasis* and is identical with the universality of reconciliation. The other way is that of renewed reflection on the seriousness of the human decision which, according to the overwhelming testimony of Scripture, is associated with the *kerygma* that goes out to the world.[253]

Brunner teaches that there is a dialectical unity of Holiness and Love. The Bible teaches the doctrine of the holy and merciful God, who in Jesus Christ has chosen all who believe in Him from all eternity, but who rejects those who refuse this obedience of faith. It is on this basis that he criticizes Barth's doctrine of Election.[254]

Universalism has been taught by many groups both within and outside the Church. Many theologians both in the past and in the present tend toward Universalism. Barth differs from them all on the basis of his christological understanding of Election. Francis Pieper taught that there is no Predestination to damnation.[255] Paul Tillich is close to Barth when he says that the doctrine of an absolutely opposite eternal destiny of individuals cannot be defended in view of both the self-manifestation of God and the nature of man.[256] Even Brunner finally arrives at the position of maintaining both the Last Judgment and universal salvation.[257] Farrelly, a Roman Catholic scholar, states that God wills mankind as a whole to reach the end of eternal life and that this is contained in the Old Testament teaching on the universal extension of the kingdom of God and in the New Testament doctrine of the Church's Commission by Christ to expand his mission to all nations as well as in the affirmation of the universality of God's salvific will that all men should be saved.[258]

Teilhard de Chardin speaks of Christ as the only saved Man. He has a strong preference for an Origenistic Universalism. He prefers this on evolutionary grounds.[259] He, however, believes in the possibility of man's own eternal damnation.[260] Loraine Boettner says that so far as the principles of sovereignty and personal election are concerned there is no reason why a Calvinist might not hold that all men will finally be saved and some Calvinists have actually held this view.[261] Walter Marshall Horton says that there are difficulties both in Universalism and eternal punishment and asserts that no outcome of the cosmic drama is acceptable that denies God's eternal opposition to evil.[262]

Oscar Cullmann introduces the principle of representation into the doctrine of Election. This is the Election of a minority for the redemption of the whole. In the Old Testament there is a reduction from the World to Israel, from Israel to the Remnant. In the New Testament there is a progression from Jesus Christ, to the Church and from the Church to redeemed humanity.[263]

Modern theology has been moving in the direction of Universalism. Barth is more christologically oriented than others. The Eastern Orthodox churches have always leaned in this direction. They have always repudiated a legalistic type of Predestination. The theology of Eastern Orthodox is also one that proclaims that Jesus is Victor. Barth's christological Universalism is in good company. Lutheranism teaches the universality of God's grace and Calvinism the sovereignty of God's grace. Does not the whole of theology, ancient and modern, teach the triumph of God over evil?

2. *Problem of the relation of Faith to Election.*

How does faith fit into the view of Jesus Christ as the

only Man rejected by God? Berkouwer points out that the tension in Barth's doctrine of Election arises from the relationship between universal election and human decision.[264] Matczak says that the problem of personal belief still lacks clarity in Barth's explanation of unbelief as a paradox because the Bible requires a personal, subjective belief for our eternal salvation.[265]

Barth emphasizes the necessity of faith to escape the judgment of God.[266] In faith we look to God who lives for us.[267] God's life for us is our deliverance from judgment. This is the faithfulness of God toward us.[268] The situation of Faith is one of looking at the objectivity of God's decision and act rather than at our own unfaithfulness and possibility of being lost. There is a placing of the objectivity of God's decision and act above that of man's subjective response.

The evidence before us of our salvation is Jesus Christ who already was rejected in our place and for us according to the eternal decree of God executed in time and history. This is what really counts in the final analysis. Man's unbelief cannot annul the fact that God has decreed our salvation. Unbelief itself is rejected and has no eternal ontological status. God's concrete decree, Jesus Christ as the rejected and the Elect, means that ultimately all will acknowledge and confess this truth, Philippians 2:9-11; Revelation 1:7.

3. *The problem of Election and the existential side of sin.*

If Jesus Christ is the only Man rejected by God what is the significance of the existential side of sin, unbelief, impenitence? Barth has spoken of the ontological impossibility of sin. For this reason sin is a mystery. Berkouwer contends that if sin is ontologically impossible then a transition from wrath to grace in the historical sphere is no longer thinkable.[269]

Jensen points out Barth's rejection of Neo-Protestantism's view of sin. In this view sin becomes the conflict in a drama which would not be complete without it. It achieves a relative necessity in God's plan for man's development. To Barth this is false doctrine.[270] Sin is not willed by God at all. Sin cannot be captured in thought but only overcome in action.[271]

There is an existential side to evil in Barth's system. Sin is the negative reaction to God's forgiving grace in Jesus Christ. It is man's attempt to behave as if he were not reconciled to God through Jesus Christ.[272] Man's pride is his refusal to be saved by Jesus Christ. Sin is unbelief in Jesus Christ.[273]

Man's inertia is the attempt to behave as if Jesus Christ were not risen and to continue in the old ruts.[274] Man's untruthfulness is also his sin. Man denies the truth that Christ has redeemed him.[275]

There is a limitation of sin and evil. It cannot produce a kingdom alongside of God the Creator and Reconciler.[276] There is no eternal Dualism.[277]

Unbelief and impenitence cannot be eternal; they are ontologically impossible. They have no basis in themselves. They are related to the grace of God. They are what God has not willed.

The only point in the whole of Barth's doctrine of Election which seems almost irreconcilable with the thesis that Jesus Christ is the only Man rejected by God is Barth's refusal to identify this with universal reconciliation and to speak only of the possibility of the salvation of all men as we look to the decree of God identical with the Person and work of Jesus Christ.

Barth's christological methodology opens up new possibilities in the area of Dogmatics and Theology. Its practical significance for the life of the Church is as follows:

a. Pastoral Concern: To the troubled conscience, to the man who feels that he is eternally lost because of his sin, his doubts or inability to accept the Gospel of Jesus Christ or be a member of the Church, there is christological assurance. God's decree and decision is superior to man's response or sin or unbelief. There is greater certainty of one's own eternal salvation or personal destiny if one accepts Barth's christological methodology.

b. Evangelism and mission work: There will be greater enthusiasm in preaching the Gospel of Jesus Christ—greater emphasis in what Christ has done for us rather than what we have to do. One will preach on the defeat of sin as the primary emphasis rather than on sin as a reality, on eternal salvation as a primary emphasis rather than on eternal damnation.

c. Parish Preaching: The emphasis will not be on the gloomy message of the Law, of man's sin and guilt, of his doom and of the wrath and judgment of God, on pessimism, but all of this will be included and subordinate to the victory of God over sin. There will be greater optimism in the pulpit as this concept is applied to the social, moral and political problems of the day.

d. Pastoral Work: This will lead to the elimination of judging others on the basis of their theological beliefs or their moral behaviour or denominational affiliation. This will lead further to the elimination of judging or condemning delinquent or inactive members of the Church and this will eliminate the refusal to bury unbelievers, godless people or inactive members of the Church because such people are christologically understood as people whose rejection has been rejected and who are also elected in Christ. As people on the left hand of God they are rejected but as people on the right hand of God they are accepted.

e. Denominationalism: This will not eliminate the institutional Church or denominationalism but it will not see salvation as based on membership in these organizations but rather in the Election and rejection of Jesus Christ.

f. Ecumenical Movement: There will be greater striving to express our unity as the Body elected in Christ. God has elected the Church, not individual denominations. The Church is not primarily a hierarchical structure of the clergy distinct from the laity, not a form of ecclesiastical government (Episcopal, Presbyterian, Congregational), not a denomination with particular liturgical rites and customs, forms of worship, creeds, confessions and doctrines. The Church is primarily the elect people of God, the reconciled and redeemed people of God. On this side of the grave and eternity it consists of those who acknowledge their Election in Jesus Christ, on the other side of the grave and eternity the Church Triumphant in Heaven is redeemed humanity. The Church must be christologically understood. In Christ God has elected mankind for community with Himself. In Jesus Christ mankind is reconciled to God and redeemed.

g. Life of Sanctification: If we see the impossibility of

sin and that the grace of God is the only reality, then we will strive to express our being elected in Christ in faith and Christian living because the rejection of Jesus Christ means the rejection of the old man of sin and the way of sin.

Barth's christological methodology opens up new horizons in the life of the Church: in systematic and practical theology.

NOTES

1. Herbert Hartwell, *The Theology of Karl Barth—An Introduction* (Philadelphia: The Westminster Press, 1964), p. 15-16.
2. Karl Barth, *Church Dogmatics,* Vol. II, *The Doctrine of God,* ed. G. W. Bromiley and T. F. Torrance, trans. G. W. Bromiley, et. al. (Edinburgh: T & T. Clark, 1957), Part II, p. 3.
3. R. Garrigou-Lagrange, *Predestination,* trans. Dom Bede, 1939 (St. Louis, Mo. and London: B. Herder Book Co., 1950), p. 24.
4. *Ibid.,* p. 25.
5. Barth, *op. cit.,* p. 46.
6. *Ibid.,* p. 45.
7. *Ibid.,* p. 80
8. *Ibid.,* p. 77
9. *Ibid.,* p. 78
10. *Ibid.*
11. *Ibid.,* pp. 80-81.
12. *Ibid.,* p. 81.
13. *Ibid.,* p. 84.
14. *Ibid.,* pp. 84-89.
15. Francis Pieper, *Church Dogmatics,* Vol. III (St. Louis, Mo.: Concordia Publishing House, 153), pp. 419 ff.
16. Barth, *op. cit.,* pp. 82-83.
17. *Ibid.,* p. 76.
18. *Ibid.,* p. 49
19. *Ibid.,* p. 51.
20. *Ibid.,* pp. 76-77.
21. *Ibid.,* p. 54.
22. *Ibid.,* p. 90.
23. Loraine Boettner, *The Reformed Doctrine of Predestination* (Philadelphia, Pa.: The Presbyterian and Reformed Publishing Co., 1966), p. 5.

24. *Ibid.*, p. 47.
25. *Ibid.*, p. 47.
26. *Ibid.*, pp. 48-49.
27. Barth, *op. cit.*, p. 149.
28. *Ibid.*, pp. 149-150.
29. *Ibid.*, p. 150.
30. *Ibid.*, pp. 109-110.
31. Emil Brunner, *The Christian Doctrine of God-Dogmatics,* Vol. I, trans. Olive Wyon (Philadelphia: The Westminster Press, 1950), p. 341.
32. St. Augustine, "On the Predestination of the Saints," *A Select Library of the Nicene and Post-Nicene Fathers of the Christian Church,* ed. Philip Schaff (Grand Rapids, Mich.: Wm. B. Eerdmans Publishing Co., 1956), Vol. V, p. 512.
33. Barth, *op. cit.*, p. 16.
34. *Ibid.*, p. 16.
35. George S. Faber, *The Primitive Doctrine of Election* (New York: D. Appleton & Co., 1843), p. xiv, preface.
36. *Ibid.*, p. 33.
37. *Ibid.*, p. 113.
38. H. Richard Niebuhr, *Christ and Culture* (New York: Harper & Bros., 1951), p. 217.
39. Barth, *op. cit.*, pp. 106-107.
40. *Ibid.*, p. 107.
41. *Ibid.*, p. 107.
42. *Ibid.*, p. 108.
43. *Ibid.*, p. 119.
44. *Ibid.*, pp. 119-120.
45. *Ibid.*, pp. 16-17.
46. Thomas Aquinas, *The Summa Theologica,* trans. Fathers of the English Dominican Province, rev. Daniel U. Sullivan (Chicago, London, Toronto: William Benton), Vol. I, p. 133.
47. *Ibid.*, p. 134.
48. *Ibid.*, p. 134.
49. *Ibid.*, p. 134.
50. *Ibid.*, pp. 134-135.
51. Dom M. John Farrelly, *Predestination, Grace, and Free Will* (Westminster, Md.: The Newman Press, 1964), pp. 10-11.
52. Barth, *op. cit.*, pp. 65-66.

53. John Dillenberger, *God Hidden and Revealed* (Philadelphia: Muhlenberg Press, 1953), pp. 109-110.
54. *Ibid.*, p. 110.
55. Barth, *op. cit.*, p. 66.
56. *Ibid.*, p. 66.
57. Martin Luther, *Bondage of the Will,* trans. J. I. Packer and O. R. Johnston (Westwood, N.J.: Fleming H. Revell Co., 1957), p. 170.
58. *Ibid.*, pp. 175-176.
59. *Ibid.*, p. 176.
60. Barth, *op. cit.*, p. 17.
61. J. L. Neve, *A History of Christian Thought,* Vol. I (Philadelphia: The Muhlenberg Press, 1946), p. 245.
62. Barth, *op. cit.*, p. 111.
63. *Ibid.*, p. 17.
64. John Calvin, *Institutes of the Christian Religion,* Vol. II, trans. John Allen (7th ed. rev.; Philadelphia: Presbyterian Board of Christian Education), p. 176.
65. *Ibid.*, p. 181.
66. *Ibid.*, p. 203.
67. *Ibid.*, p. 232.
68. John Calvin, *Calvin's Calvinism,* trans. Henry Cole (Grand Rapids, Mich.: Wm. B. Eerdmans Pub. Co., 1950), p. 81.
69. *Ibid.*, p. 92.
70. Boettner, *op. cit.*, p. 105.
71. Brunner, *op. cit.*, p. 325.
72. Calvin, *Institutes of the Christian Religion,* pp. 223-224.
73. Calvin, *Calvin's Calvinism,* p. 111.
74. *Ibid.*, p. 16.
75. *Ibid.*, p. 133.
76. Barth, *op. cit.*, p. 112.
77. *Ibid.*, p. 127.
78. *Ibid.*, p. 128.
79. *Ibid.*
80. *Ibid.*, p. 129.
81. *Ibid.*, pp. 129-130.
82. *Ibid.*
83. *Ibid.*, pp. 130-131.
84. *Ibid.*, p. 131.
85. *Ibid.*

86. *Ibid.*, p. 134.
87. *Ibid.*
88. *Ibid.*, p. 67.
89. *Ibid.*
90. *Ibid.*, pp. 67-68.
91. *Ibid.*, p. 68.
92. Karl Barth, *Church Dogmatics,* Vol. IV, *The Doctrine of Reconciliation,* ed. G. W. Bromiley and T. F. Torrance, trans. G. W. Bromiley (Edinburgh: T. & T. Clark, 1956), Part I, p. 54.
93. *Ibid.*, pp. 57-58.
94. *Ibid.*
95. *Ibid.*, pp. 59-60.
96. *Ibid.*, pp. 64-65.
97. *Ibid.*, pp. 65-66.
98. Barth, *Church Dogmatics,* Vol. II, *The Doctrine of God,* Part II, pp. 70-71.
99. *Ibid.*, p. 71.
100. *Ibid.*, pp. 72-73.
101. *Ibid.*
102. *Ibid.*, p. 75.
103. *Ibid.*
104. *Ibid.*, p. 112.
105. *Ibid.*, p. 146.
106. Karl Barth, *The Humanity of God* (Richmond, Va.: John Knox Press, 1964), pp. 46-47.
107. Barth, *Church Dogmatics,* Vol. IV, *The Doctrine of Reconciliation,* Part I, pp. 204-205.
108. *Ibid.*, p. 203.
109. Jerome Hamer, *Karl Barth,* trans. Dominic M. Maruca, S.J. (Westminster, Md.: The Newman Press, 1962), p. 165.
110. Barth, *Church Dogmatics,* Vol. II, *The Doctrine of God,* Part II, p. 104.
111. *Ibid.*, pp. 101-102.
112. Karl Barth, *Dogmatics In Outline* (New York, Evanston, London: Harper and Row, Publishers, 1959), p. 65.
113. Barth, *Church Dogmatics,* Vol. IV, *The Doctrine of Reconciliation,* Part I, pp. 203-204.
114. Barth, *Church Dogmatics,* Vol. II, *The Doctrine of God,* Part II, pp. 107-108.

115. *Ibid.*, p. 115.
116. *Ibid.*, p. 116.
117. *Ibid.*, pp. 116-117.
118. *Ibid.*, p. 118.
119. *Ibid.*, p. 120.
120. Barth, *Church Dogmatics*, Vol. IV, *The Doctrine of Reconciliation*, Part I, p. 53.
121. *Ibid.*
122. Barth, *Church Dogmatics*, Vol. II, *The Doctrine of God*, Part II, p. 94.
123. *Ibid.*, p. 158.
124. *Ibid.*, p. 162.
125. Karl Barth, *The Epistle to the Romans*, trans. Edwyn C. Hoskyns (6th ed.; London: Oxford University Press, 1933), pp. 333-334.
126. *Ibid.*, p. 346.
127. *Ibid.*, pp. 347-348.
128. *Ibid.*, pp. 352-353.
129. *Ibid.*, p. 402.
130. Barth, *Church Dogmatics*, Vol. II, *The Doctrine of God*, Part II, pp. 162-163.
131. *Ibid.*, p. 164.
132. *Ibid.*, p. 166.
133. *Ibid.*, pp. 171-172.
134. *Ibid.*, pp. 174-175.
135. Barth, *The Epistle to the Romans*, p. 181.
136. *Ibid.*, 182.
137. Barth, *Church Dogmatics*, Vol. II, *The Doctrine of God*, Part II, pp. 318-319.
138. *Ibid.*, p. 346.
139. *Ibid.*, p. 352.
140. *Ibid.*, pp. 352-353.
141. Barth, *Church Dogmatics*, Vol. IV, *The Doctrine of Reconciliation*, Part I, pp. 242-243.
142. Barth, *Church Dogmatics*, Vol. II, *The Doctrine of God*, Part II, pp. 122-123.
143. *Ibid.*, p. 123.
144. *Ibid.*, p. 453.
145. *Ibid.*, p. 450.
146. Karl Barth, *Church Dogmatics*, Vol. II, *The Doctrine of God*, ed. G. W. Bromiley and T. F. Torrance, trans.

T. H. L. Parker, et al. (Edinburgh: T. & T. Clark, 1957), Part I, pp. 373-374.

147. *Ibid.*, p. 396.
148. *Ibid.*, p. 400.
149. Karl Barth, *Church Dogmatics*, Vol. III, *The Doctrine of Creation*, ed. G. W. Bromiley and T. F. Torrance, trans. G. W. Bromiley, et al. (Edinburgh: T. & T. Clark, 1961), Part III, p. 349.
150. *Ibid.*, pp. 354-355.
151. *Ibid.*, p. 354.
152. *Ibid.*, pp. 351-352.
153. *Ibid.*, p. 358.
154. *Ibid.*, p. 362.
155. John Hick, *Evil And The God of Love* (New York: Harper and Row, Publishers, 1966), p. 141.
156. *Ibid.*, p. 142.
157. *Ibid.*, p. 142.
158. *Ibid.*, pp. 148-149.
159. *Ibid.*, p. 149.
160. Barth, *Church Dogmatics*, Vol. III, *The Doctrine of Creation*, Part III, p. 305.
161. *Ibid.*, pp. 305-306.
162. *Ibid.*, pp. 352-353.
163. Herbert Hartwell, *The Theology of Karl Barth, An Introduction* (Philadelphia: The Westminster Press, 1964), pp. 122-123.
164. Barth, *Church Dogmatics*, Vol. IV, *The Doctrine of Reconciliation*, Part I, p. 194.
165. *Ibid.*, p. 195.
166. Barth, *Church Dogmatics*, Vol. II, *The Doctrine of God*, Part II, pp. 186-187.
167. Barth, *Epistle to the Romans*, pp. 62-66, 184-185.
168. Fred H. Klooster, *The Significance of Barth Theology, An Appraisal: With Special Reference to Election and Reconciliation* (Grand Rapids, Michigan: Baker Book House, 1961), p. 70.
169. H. H. Rowley, *The Biblical Doctrine of Election* (London: Lutterworth Press, 1950), pp. 41-42.
170. Barth, *Church Dogmatics*, Vol. IV, *The Doctrine of Reconciliation*, Part I, p. 541.
171. *Ibid.*, pp. 548-549.

172. *Ibid.*, p. 550.
173. Barth, *Church Dogmatics,* Vol. III, *The Doctrine of Creation,* Part III, p. 355.
174. Barth, *Church Dogmatics,* Vol. IV, *The Doctrine of Reconciliation,* Part I, pp. 89-90.
175. Barth, *The Epistle to the Romans,* pp. 383-384.
176. *Ibid.*, p. 384.
177. *Ibid.*, pp. 395-396.
178. Barth, *Church Dogmatics,* Vol. II, *The Doctrine of God,* Part II, pp. 417-418.
179. *Ibid.*, p. 422.
180. *Ibid.*
181. *Ibid.*, p. 423.
182. *Ibid.*, p. 476.
183. *Ibid.*, p. 477.
184. *Ibid.*, p. 495.
185. *Ibid.*, p. 495.
186. *Ibid.*, p. 496.
187. *Ibid.*
188. *Ibid.*
189. Barth, *The Humanity of God,* pp. 90-91.
190. Barth, *Church Dogmatics,* Vol. II, *The Doctrine of God,* pp. 90-91.
191. *Ibid.*, p. 38.
192. Barth, *The Humanity of God,* p. 89.
193. Karl Barth, *Church Dogmatics,* Vol. IV, *The Doctrine of Reconciliation,* ed. G. W. Bromiley and T. F. Torrance, trans. G. W. Bromiley (Edinburgh: T. & T. Clark, 1961), Part III, 1st half, pp. 174-175.
194. Emil Brunner, *The Christian Doctrine of the Church, Faith and the Consummation, Dogmatics,* Vol. III, trans. David Cairus and T. H. L. Parker (Philadelphia: The Westminster Press, 1960), p, 417.
195. Barth, *Church Dogmatics,* Vol. IV, *The Doctrine of Reconciliation,* Part III, 1st half, p. 173.
196. Jacob Jocz, *A Theology of Election: Israel and the Church* (London: S.P.C.K., 1958), p. 156.
197. *Ibid.*, p. 159.
198. Barth, *The Humanity of God,* pp. 92-93.
199. Barth, *Church Dogmatics,* Vol. IV, *The Doctrine of Reconciliation,* Part III, 1st half, p. 465.
200. *Ibid.*, p. 477.

201. *Ibid.*, pp. 477-478.
202. Cornelius Van Til, *Christianity and Barthianism* (Grand Rapids: Baker Book House, 1962), p. 49.
203. *Ibid.*, p. 108.
204. Hartwell, *The Theology of Karl Barth—An Introduction*, p. 30.
205. *Ibid.*, p. 23.
206. Barth, *The Humanity of God*, pp. 93-94.
207. *Ibid.*, p. 95.
208. Barth, *Church Dogmatics*, Vol. II, *The Doctrine of God*, Part II, p. 148.
209. *Ibid.*, pp. 96-97.
210. *Ibid.*, p. 99.
211. *Ibid.*, p. 117.
212. *Ibid.*, p. 106.
213. *Ibid.*, p. 148.
214. *Ibid.*, p. 60.
215. *Ibid.*, pp. 299-300.
216. *Ibid.*, p. 300.
217. Brunner, *The Christian Doctrine of God-Dogmatics*, Vol. I, p. 314.
218. *Ibid.*, p. 315.
219. *Ibid.*, p. 318.
220. *Ibid.*, p. 232.
221. Barth, *Church Dogmatics*, Vol. II, *The Doctrine of God*, Part II, p. 486.
222. Cornelius Van Til, *Christianity and Barthianism* (Grand Rapids, Mich.: Baker Book House, 1962), pp. 108-109.
223. Gordon H. Clark, *Karl Barth's Theological Method* (Philadelphia: The Presbyterian and Reformed Publishing Co., 1963), p. 165.
224. Van Til, *Christianity and Barthianism*, pp. 164-165, 170.
225. St. Augustine, "On Rebuke and Grace," *A Select Library of the Nicene and Post-Nicene Fathers of the Christian Church*, ed. Philip Schaff (Grand Rapids, Mich.: Wm. B. Eerdmans Publishing Co., 1956), Vol. V, pp. 489-491.
226. Calvin, *Calvin's Calvinism*, p. 275.
227. Boettner, *op. cit.*, pp. 287-288.
228. *Ibid.*, 288.

229. *Ibid.*, 290.
230. *Ibid.*, p. 291.
231. *Ibid.*, pp. 291-292.
232. *Ibid.*, p. 296.
233. Barth, *Church Dogmatics,* Vol. IV, *The Doctrine of Reconciliation,* Part I, p. 157.
234. *Ibid.*, p. 165.
235. *Ibid.*, p. 177.
236. *Ibid.*, p. 184.
237. *Ibid.*, 185.
238. *Ibid.*
239. *Ibid.*, pp. 94-95.
240. *Ibid.*, pp. 222-223.
241. *Ibid.*, pp. 236-237.
242. *Ibid.*, p. 242.
243. *Ibid.*, pp. 253-254.
244. *Ibid.*, p. 259.
245. *Ibid.*, p. 298.
246. *Ibid.*, p. 217.
247. O. Weber, *Karl Barth's Church Dogmatics, An Introductory Report on Vol. I-III,* trans. A. C. Cochrane (1953), pp. 101-102.
248. Hartwell, *op. cit.*, p. 111.
249. Sebastian A. Matczak, *Karl Barth on God: The Knowledge of the Divine Existence* (New York: St. Paul Publications, 1962), pp. 167-168.
250. Van Til, *op. cit.*, p. 32.
251. *Ibid.*, p. 445.
252. Berkouwer, *op. cit.*, p. 266.
253. *Ibid.*, p. 290.
254. Brunner, *The Christian Doctrine of God,* Vol. I, p. 337.
255. Pieper, *op. cit.*, p. 498.
256. Paul Tillich, *Systematic Theology,* Vol. III (The University of Chicago Press, 1963), p. 407.
257. Brunner, *The Christian Doctrine of the Church, Faith, and the Consummation,* pp. 421-422.
258. Farrelly, *op. cit.*, p. 300.
259. Michael H. Murray, *The Thought of Teilhard de Chardin: An Introduction* (New York: The Seabury Press, 1966), p. 101.
260. *Ibid.*, p. 104.
261. Boettner, *op. cit.*, p. 131.

262. Walter Marshall Horton, *Christian Theology—An Ecumenical Approach* (New York: Harper and Brothers Publishers, 1958), pp. 268-269.
263. Oscar Cullmann, *Christ and Time,* trans. Floyd Filson (Philadelphia: The Westminster Press, 1950), pp. 115-117.
264. Berkouwer, *op. cit.,* p. 288.
265. Matczak, *op. cit.,* p. 167.
266. Barth, *Church Dogmatics,* Vol. II, *The Doctrine of God,* Part I, p. 392.
267. *Ibid.,* pp. 392-393.
268. *Ibid.,* p. 393.
269. Berkouwer, *op. cit.,* p. 233.
270. Robert W. Jensen, *Alpha and Omega—A Study in the Theology of Karl Barth* (Edinburgh: Thomas Nelson and Sons, 1963), p. 44.
271. *Ibid.,* 45.
272. *Ibid.,* p. 37.
273. *Ibid.*
274. *Ibid.,* pp. 37-38.
275. *Ibid.,* p. 38.
276. *Ibid.,* p. 39.
277. *Ibid.*

BIBLIOGRAPHY

I. The Works of Karl Barth

Church Dogmatics, Vol. II, *The Doctrine of God,* Edited by G. W. Bromiley and T. F. Torrance. Translated by T.H. L. Parker, W. B. Johnston, Harold Knight, J.L.M. Haire. Edinburgh: T. & T. Clark, 1957. First Half-Volume. 699 pages.

Church Dogmatics, Vol. II, *The Doctrine of God.* Edited by G. W. Bromiley and T. F. Torrance. Translated by G. W. Bromiley, J. C. Campbell, Iain Wilson, J. Strathearn McNab, Harold Knight, R. A. Stewart. Edinburgh: T. & T. Clark, 1957. Second Half-Volume, 806 pages.

Church Dogmatics, Vol. III, *The Doctrine of Creation.* Edited by G. W. Bromiley and T. F. Torrance. Translated by G. W. Bromiley and R. J. Ehrlich. Edinburgh: T. & T. Clark, 1961. Part 3. 544 pages.

Church Dogmatics, Vol. IV, *The Doctrine of Reconciliation.* Edited by G. W. Bromiley and T. F. Torrance. Translated by G. W. Bromiley. Edinburgh: T. & T. Clark, 1961. Part 1. 802 pages.

Church Dogmatics, Vol. IV, *The Doctrine of Reconciliation.* Edited by G. W. Bromiley and T. F. Torrance. Translated by G. W. Bromiley. Edinburgh: T. & T. Clark, 1962. Part 3, Second Half. 963 pages.

Church Dogmatics, Vol. IV, *The Doctrine of Reconciliation.* Edited by G. W. Bromiley and T. F. Torrance. Translated by G. W. Bromiley. Edinburgh: T. & T. Clark, 1961. Part 3, First Half. 478 pages.

Dogmatics in Outline. Translated by G. T. Thomson. New York: Harper and Row, Publishers, 1959. 155 pages.

The Epistle to the Romans. Translated from the 6th edition by Edwyn C. Hoskyns. London: Oxford University Press, 1933. 547 pages.

The Humanity of God. Translated by Thomas Wieser. Richmond: John Knox Press, 1964. 96 pages.

II. Category of Works on the Theology of Karl Barth

Berkouwer, G. C. *The Triumph of Grace in the Theology of Karl Barth.* Translated from the Dutch by Harry R. Boer. Grand Rapids: Wm. B. Eerdman Publishing Co., 1956. 414 pages.

Brunner, Emil. *The Christian Doctrine of God-Dogmatics.* Vol. I. Translated by Olive Wyon. Philadelphia: The Westminster Press, 1950. 361 pages.

Clark, Gordon H. *Karl Barth's Theological Method.* Philadelphia: The Presbyterian and Reformed Publishing Co., 1963. 229 pages.

Hamer, Jerome. *Karl Barth.* Translated by Dominic M. Maruca. Westminster, Md.: The Newman Press, 1962. 300 pages.

Hartwell, Herbert. *The Theology of Karl Barth—An Introduction.* Philadelphia: The Westminster Press, 1964. 201 pages.

Klooster, Fred H. *The Significance of Barth's Theology, An Appraisal: With Special Reference to Election and Reconciliation.* Grand Rapids: Baker Book House, 1961. 98 pages.

Matczak, Sebastian A. *Karl Barth on God: The Knowledge of the Divine Existence.* New York: St. Paul Publications, 1962. 358 pages.

Jensen, Robert W. *Alpha and Omega—A Study in the Theology of Karl Barth.* Edinburgh: Thomas Nelson and Sons, 1963. 175 pages.

Weber, O. *Karl Barth's Church Dogmatics, An Introductory Report on Vol. I, I to III, 4.* Translated by A. C. Cochrane, 1953. 253 pages.

Van Til, Cornelius. *Christianity and Barthianism.* Grand Rapids: Baker Book House, 1962. 450 pages.

III. Category of Works on Predestination in General

Aquinas, Thomas. *The Summa Theologica.* Translated by the Fathers of the English Dominican Province. Revised by Daniel J. Sullivan. Vol. I. Chicago: William Benton, Publisher, Encyclopaedia Britannica.

Boettner, Loraine. *The Reformed Doctrine of Predestination.* Philadelphia: The Presbyterian and Reformed Publishing Company, 1966. 440 pages.

Brunner, Emil. *The Christian Doctrine of the Church, Faith, and the Consummation, Dogmatics,* Vol. III. Translated by David Cairus and T. H. L. Parker. Philadelphia: The Westminster Press, 1960. 457 pages.

Calvin, John. *Institutes of Christian Religion,* Vol. II. Translated from the Latin and Collated with the Author's Last Edition in French by John Allen. 7th American Edition, revised and corrected. Philadelphia: Presbyterian Board of Christian Education. 812 pages.

Calvin, John. *Calvin's Calvinism.* Original title: *De Aeterna Del Praedestinatione.* Translated into English by Henry Cole. Grand Rapids: W. B. Eerdmans Publishing Co., 1950. 350 pages.

Cullmann, Oscar. *Christ and Time.* Translated from the German by Floyd V. Filson. Philadelphia: The Westminster Press, 1950. 253 pages.

Dillenberger, John. *God Hidden and Revealed.* Philadelphia: Muhlenberg Press, 1953. 193 pages.

Faber, George S. *The Primitive Doctrine of Election.* New York: D. Appleton & Co., 1843. 376 pages.

Farrelly, Dom M. John. *Predestination, Grace and Free Will.* Westminster, Md.: The Newman Press, 1964. 317 pages.

Garrigou-Lagrange, R. *Predestination.* Translated by Dom. Bede. St. Louis, Mo.: B. Herder Book Co., 1950. 382 pages.

Hick, John. *Evil and the God of Love.* New York: Harper and Row, Publishers, 1966. 403 pages.

Horton, Walter Marshall. *Christian Theology—An Ecumenical Approach.* New York: Harper and Brothers, Publishers, 1958. 320 pages.

Jocz, Jacob. *A Theology of Election: Israel and the Church.* London: S. P. C. K., 1958. 227 pages.

Luther, Martin. *The Bondage of the Will.* Translated by J. I. Packer and O. R. Johnston. Westwood, N.J.: Fleming H. Revell Co., 1957. 322 pages.

Murray, Michael H. *The Thought of Teilhard de Chardin: An Introduction.* New York: The Seabury Press, 1966. 177 pages.

Neve, J. L. *A History of Christian Thought,* Vol. I. Philadelphia: The Muhlenberg Press, 1946. 344 pages.

Niebuhr, H. Richard. *Christ and Culture.* New York: Harper and Brothers, Publishers, 1951. 256 pages.

Pieper, Francis. *Church Dogmatics,* Vol. III. St. Louis: Concordia Publishing House, 1953. 555 pages.

Rowley, H. H. *The Biblical Doctrine of Election.* London: Lutterworth Press, 1950. 184 pages.

St. Augustine. *A Select Library of the Nicene and Post-Nicene Fathers of the Christian Church,* Vol. V. Edited by Philip Schaff. Grand Rapids: Wm. B. Eerdmans Publishing Co., 1956. 567 pages.

Tillich, Paul. *Systematic Theology,* Vol. III. *Life and the Spirit, History and the Kingdom of God.* University of Chicago Press, 1963. 434 pages.